90p.

the action starts here...

TOP
OF THE
POPS

**Edited by
KEN IRWIN**

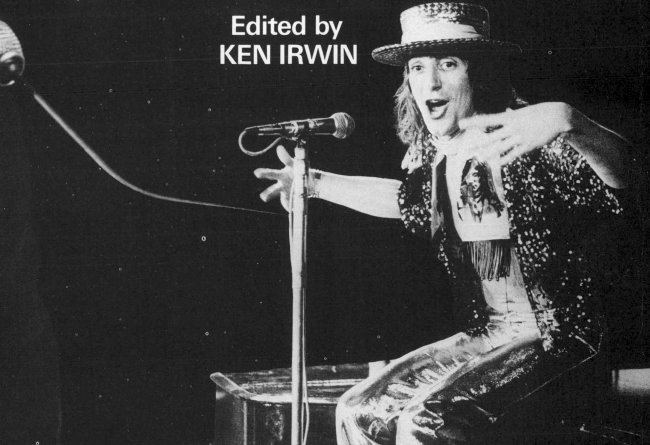

OUR THANKS TO

We would like to thank all Agents, Publicists, TV and Record Companies for permission to reproduce some of the photographs in this book. Their co-operation is very much appreciated. Thanks also go to photographer Crispian Woodgate and Brian Clifford of the BBC, and to Gay Robertson and Paula Leonard of the BBC for their valuable co-operation and assistance.
For kind permission to reprint photographs, we especially thank:

A & M Records
ATV
BBC
Bell Records
CBS Records
Decca Records

EMI
Island Records
London Weekend TV
MAM
Mercury Records
Penny Farthing Records

Phonogram
Leslie Perrin Associates
Polydor Records
RCA Records
Thames TV
Tony Barrow International
Tony Brainsby Publicity

contents

Welcome...

Well, here we are . . . eleven years of non-stop Top of the Pops!

The programme goes into its second decade – to create a new record in television history.

From such a humble beginning – in a tiny church-hall studio in Manchester in January 1964 – Top of the Pops has now become the undisputed No. 1 pop show on television. Probably No. 1 throughout the world – because even in America there is no nationwide show which promotes pure pop as this programme does.

How has it managed to stay so successful? And for so long? For the answer to that, I suppose, we have to ask someone who has been with it right from the outset.

Like Jimmy Savile, the original deejay who presented the very first programme. Says Jim: "It's survived because it's the greatest show – that's why!

"We give the punters – the viewers out there – the kind of music they want. We only reflect their tastes in pop music."

But what is "pop" exactly?

Pop, dear readers, is everything in music which is popular. From Gilbert O'Sullivan and Cliff Richard . . . to the Osmonds, David Cassidy and Dave Bowie.

From the zing-and-zany musical talent of Roy Wood . . . to the thumping *noize* of Slade.

From Perry Como and "old-timers" like him . . . to groups who really get stuck in – like Mud, and Sweet, and the Stones.

Pop is also dancing . . . the funky dancing of Pan's People . . . the movement and body rhythms of the Detroit Emeralds and the Jacksons . . . the slinky sexiness of the Supremes . . . the gyrations of Wizzard.

On average, 12 million viewers tune in to watch Top of the Pops on BBC-1 every week. Some weeks, that figure has even shot up to around 15 million.

Which is proof enough that the programme, as its initials suggest, is TOP.

I hope you enjoy reading this, our second *Top of the Pops Annual*.

And may I wish you happy pop-viewing in 1975.

K. Harri

JIMMY SAVILE
The Daddy of the DJs

"I think that 1975 will be one of the biggest years for Pop because it looks like this country and the world generally is going into a decline commercially. And when it comes to periods of decline, entertainment comes into its own, together with a lot of other things.

The people with jobs which will be really safe are people who work in hospitals, post offices and such. The institutionalised jobs where, in time of prosperity, the people doing them get the thin end of the wedge, and in times of stress find their jobs much sought after.

Entertainment will be bigger, because people will always find time for entertainment, and will want their minds taken off things.

You can go back through history. Once upon a time a Roman nation was faced with the situation where ships returning from Africa could bring one of two things. Either wheat from Egypt to feed the populace, or they could bring the special white sand that was laid on the floor of the Coliseum for the Games.

And the Caesar of the time realised that entertainment was vital to keep the mobs from rising. So he decreed that they should bring the white sand – for entertainment.

And if for no other reason that the pop game today is a very mobile business, it's got everything in its favour to have quite a bumper year.

Pop will have a bumper year in entertainment because pop is the easiest and the most candyfloss of all entertainment. Because the success of pop records rests on the fact that you're asking somebody for two-and-a-half minutes to forget their worries and listen to "Scoobie Doobie Doo", "Tie A Yellow Ribbon Round The Old Oak Tree", or whatever. You're not asking them to do it for two-and-a-half hours, like Bach, Beethoven or whoever.

It's such a candyfloss scene, and because we are not demanding a lot of time from people, the pop end of the entertainment business will do even better, *pro rata*, than the other more serious end of the entertainment world. Because theatres for instance might find it difficult to attract people to sit down for three hours, when people can't push their worries away for three hours. Whereas everybody's got two-and-a-half minutes to knock off and take things easy. So we're not asking a lot of the public, y'see.

I'm an easy-going geezer, but for years I've been trying to hide the fact from people that I had a few brains. If you are hampered with brains in this world, you will inevitably finish up skint.

Fortunately, over the years, I have increased my animal cunning. So I am now totally filled with animal cunning. It was only a question of time that the media, like television and radio, found

JIMMY SAVILE
The Daddy of the DJs

that under the Top of the Pops exterior of mine there happened to be a very shrewd geezer.

I fought against them finding this out. But now they've sussed me, it's too late.

Five years ago, Bill Cotton, the BBC's light entertainment boss, came to me in my dressing room at Top of the Pops, and said: "Wear a suit and get your hair cut and you can have your own TV show."

I was just about to go on the show and I was combing my hair. I just said to him, "Boss, you're about twenty-five No. 1 awards and a quarter of a million pounds too late."

So he said, "I knew I was wasting my time," and he turned and walked out.

Now, five years later Bill Cotton came to me and said, "From 1st May, you start eight weeks of your own TV show, called 'Clunk-Click'." So I said, "Certainly."

Whereupon an amazed Mr. Cotton said, "You've always said No before." And I replied, "Before, you've always *asked* me. Today, you're *telling* me."

He was staggered. Y'see, I can't get out of things when someone *tells* me to do something — can I? And it was the first time Bill Cotton had ever *told* me.

He was very surprised that I gave in so easily. I explained to him, "It's quite simple. Before you've always *asked* me. Today, you *told* me."

That was back in 1973. Last year, I did another batch of TV programmes in the "Clunk-Click" series. It's a great honour and I love it. But it's all time consuming. I only like to work one day a week. I've become so involved with life — like working at Stoke Mandeville Hospital, Leeds Infirmary and Broadmoor, and all these ancillary things that I do. That's where I meet the people in trouble. And that really is life.

The entertainment world is okay, but I was never cut out to be totally dedicated to entertaining, because I can't really entertain. I'm really the world's greatest "take-on" because I can't sing, I can't dance, I can't tell jokes, and I can't act. I can't even remember lines.

I can't really do anything. If you were to ask me to stand up on a stage and entertain for half an hour, I'd be completely lost.

I now do all kinds of different programmes — party political broadcasts, "Songs of Praise", "The Epilogue", "Savile's Travels", "Speakeasy", "Clunk-Click", religious programmes, as well as dear old Top of the Pops.

They're all life, all a fabric of life, and I enjoy them all. It's rather like the colours in a suit, they're woven into the cloth. And if you took the blue out of the suit, then the whole garment would fall to pieces.

Well, if you took Top of the Pops away, the rest of my structure would be insecure.

The deal I've got with Bill Cotton and the BBC is that when they tell me to do a programme, I will do it, providing it's always a cert that I go back on Top of the Pops. Because that is the building brick of everything else I do. It is the foundation of everything.

In a hospital, for instance, I think I can give a great deal of pleasure to patients merely by being there, and meeting them. I'll take my trolley in and wheel someone down to the X-ray department. Now before I've opened my mouth, they say, "Ooh, it's Jimmy Savile. Wait till I tell my nephews and nieces about this, they'll be mad with jealousy!" This sort of thing gives me a great thrill, naturally.

Should you ever be unfortunate enough to lie in a hospital bed, it helps to get a little light relief from a national figure. I don't go in there as some Flash Harry for seven minutes or so. I've been doing this for seven years or more, which is longer than a lot of people who work in the hospitals.

That reaction from hospital patients is fantastic. But that reaction to me stems from one thing. It doesn't stem from party political broadcasts or the epilogues I've done, it stems from the candy-floss Top of the Pops.

I never wear make-up when I'm on TV. I'm the only artist I know on TV who never, ever wears make-up in front of the cameras. So in the summer I might look all right. But in the winter, I look like a death's head. I've not got an ego thing about my looks. I don't set myself up as a sex symbol or as a handsome man.

If I wore make-up on TV I'd be on some kind of ego trip, because I'd be saying to the public, "Here I am, accept me as a good-looking feller."

But I don't give a monkey's about being a good-looking geezer. And I might be knocking on as a disc jockey, but the people out there, the kids who watch the show never question my age. They accept me for what I am.

It's also a well-known fact in the Corporation that I'm a lot better at this job of compering Top of the Pops than anyone else they've ever had on the show, that's for sure. Because I understand all the technicalities of it by now. I'm a very obedient worker, and they have no trouble with me at all.

I'll let you into a little secret. Nothing ever upsets me. Ever. I've never in my life lost my temper. Never. I'm far too rational a person. Because when I get faced with an awkward situation, I always rationalise it.

I find I'm incapable of ever losing my temper. Some people say how boring life must be, never losing your temper. I've got news for them — it's fantastic. At all times, you're totally sober. At all times, you're in command of the situation, generally speaking.

Another little secret. I got past needing the money years ago. It's ten years or more that I stopped working. Financially, there's been no problems for me.

I've taken on all sorts of different programmes, and the cash never worries me. Often I don't even know how much they're paying me to do a show. Honest.

The man who does all the contracts for the BBC rings me up before a programme to talk about the money. I invariably say, "I'll leave it to you. It doesn't really matter." In all the years I've been working for the BBC, I've never ever even remotely had to haggle about money. What I get in cash, I get.

It just doesn't matter. It's not important to me. I've already got money. Plenty of it.

Really, the people behind the cameras on Top of the Pops are better, bigger stars than I am in front of the cameras. There's no doubt about that in my mind. All that technical jargon they talk in the director's gallery . . . well, I couldn't do any of that, I promise you.

Yet it is far more difficult than it looks, standing there, introducing a show like Top of the Pops, with lots of the kids screaming around you. That, again, is where my animal cunning comes in. I'm a great believer in animal cunning.

Animal cunning means that, short of a direct bullet through the heart, you'll always escape with the bone. And the least you can fear is a swift kick from the butcher of life. But you escape with the juicy bone.

Now I've escaped with a few juicy bones in my life. And a few kicks. But animal cunning has given me very devious footwork — 'cos I'm a great politician.

Regrets? I've none really. I wouldn't have minded this life I'm now living ten years earlier. But it doesn't really matter at all. Because, with me, the yardstick is quite simple. I've just bought myself another new Rolls-Royce. Now that's twenty grand's worth of motor car. It's a great mechanical thing.

But I'm not bothered about it being such a wonderful mechanical thing. But every time I put my backside on that seat, it's become second nature to me to see if the body that's getting into the car works as well as the car itself. And the day that the body getting into the car doesn't work as well as the car, is the day I'm going to worry.

But I keep myself fit. With lots of running and walking, and leaping about, the body that gets into that car of mine works better than the Rolls-Royce.

I climb into my car, click my seat belt, and then check that all my arms and legs are in good working order. And if ever the car won't start, it doesn't upset me in the slightest. In fact, I'm rather pleased. I say, "Good — that proves that I'm in better condition than the car."

That's the way it's got to be with me, always. If you go through life on that kind of philosophy, then nothing is a problem to you. Nothing at all.

That "Clunk-Click" safety campaign of mine gave me a great deal of personal satisfaction. We can tell from the hospitals that it has paid off. From the same amount of crashes, they've not had anything like the harvest of injuries. It's a campaign that's made a profit. A campaign which cost x number of pounds but actually made a profit in another department, in the hospital service.

On the pop scene, I have a great deal of admiration for most of these guys and gals who churn out the actual records. Y'know, I made a record about ten years ago. The only one I ever made. It was called "A-Hab the A-rab". The tune got to No. 1 in America, and over here my record sold about 13,000 copies, which was quite good actually. I gave all the money to the Little Sisters of the Poor in Leeds because I didn't want the money anyway.

I made the record for one reason. I, as a disc jockey, was playing other people's records. I just wanted to know what it felt like for a singer to have a disc jockey play his record over the air. So that my efforts as a disc jockey would bear more honesty.

And I listened to the radio, and my record got played on all sorts of programmes. And I can never forget what it was like for me to suddenly switch on the radio and hear my record being played over the air. I realised what effect that had on me. It was very valuable to me as a disc jockey. Which is why I've won so many No. 1 awards, because it changed me from being just a deejay into a disc jockey who understood the other side of the record business.

One record was enough, though. I didn't particularly want to be a singer, any more than I wanted to be an astronaut. I wanted to feel how the lads who make records felt, because this was a world I didn't understand. I do now.

The voice? It's good. I've got a pretty good voice, as it happens. I could still make a reasonable record, but I don't particularly want to.

There are many people, even in this day and age, who wish they could sell 13,000 records. It made a profit, as well. Particularly for the Little Sisters of the Poor in Leeds who were absolutely knocked out with it!"

ADDING THE CURVES TO THE POP SCENE

The girls don't often make it big in the charts in Britain. But when they do – wow! It's usually well worth waiting for.

Take three girls who have now created their own individual impact on the record-buying public. Three girls completely contrasting in personality and temperament.

Girls like Suzi Quatro, the explosive lady from America . . . and our own Olivia Newton-John . . . and Lynsey de Paul.

Suzi, the little Miss who made such a big Hit here, is certainly a girl who is different from the pack.

She fronts a swinging band – dressed in black leather jumpsuit, unzipped as daringly as decency will allow down the front – with as much zest and enthusiasm as any bloke in any other hard-working rock outfit.

Suzi did for leather jumpsuits what Gary Glitter did for Lurex!

She's a trouper. There is nothing prim and proper about her, and she has a habit of saying just what she thinks, whether it upsets people or not.

Like . . . "The whole rock scene has changed. With people like David Bowie around, there now seems to be a place for people like me."

Or . . . "I can't be bothered with make-up. I don't wear falsies or eyelashes. I don't need to."

Or, more outrageous still, she admits that she finds a great deal of sexual satisfaction in performing on stage with a guitar. "The bass guitar is a very sexy instrument to play," she says.

Suzi, now twenty-four, only five feet tall and with purple hair, doesn't worry about clothes at all. "I wear jumpsuits because on stage I jump around a lot."

She prefers trousers to skirts,

Olivia Newton-John

anyway. Off stage, she wears a T-shirt and old jeans rather than fancy dresses.

"Until recently, you had to be soft and feminine. No one wanted to know about ladies who rocked and raved," says Suzi.

The answer to that is . . . they do now.

Suzi hails from Detroit, the Tamla Motown city. She comes from a musical family, but she left home at fifteen and went off to New York on her own to join a band.

After five years of struggling in the States, she was discovered by starmaker Mickie Most, the guy who found Lulu, the Animals, Herman's Hermits and others. He was in America to see another act, but he saw Suzi instead, liked what he saw, and persuaded her to come to England.

She eventually broke through in a big way with the hit number "Can The Can" in 1973. Then she followed up with numbers like "48 Crash" and "Daytona Demon".

"It took a few years to get recognition, but I'm glad I made it the right way," she says. "If I'd been an ordinary girl singer who fluttered her eyelashes, giggled, and flashed her bust all over the TV screen, I could have had a hit record the first week I arrived in London.

"But that's not me. I'm a singer and a bass guitarist, and I want to be judged on equal terms with the guys."

If someone really wants to insult her, she says, all they have to say is something like "Suzi Quatro is a good musician – for a girl!"

She comes out very strongly against guys in her group wearing make-up. "Rock 'n' roll has all the sex appeal you need without the men having to wear lipstick," she says emphatically.

And if anyone has already conclusively proved that point, it's certainly little Miss Suzi Q.

Olivia Newton-John, on the other hand, is a complete contrast to Suzi.

She displays an entirely different sexual attraction. She's much more demure . . . and pretty, with it.

She's had some monster hits over the last few years . . . "If Not For You", "Banks Of The Ohio" and "Country Road".

And, of course, she was picked by the BBC to delicately represent Britain in the last Eurovision Song Contest, which was staged on home soil, at Brighton.

"Livvy" is a very lively girl. Pleasant to look at. Pleasant to chat to. And she has a pleasant voice to match her personality.

"But I always get terribly nervous whenever I'm performing," she says. "Particularly when I'm on TV."

She was surprised and flattered, she said, when she was singled out for the honour of appearing in the Eurovision Song Contest.

Now, she's into writing songs herself, although she doesn't read or write music. She usually sings the song on to a tape recorder, and then a musician friend puts the song down in music for her.

"I find time to write mostly when I'm in my dressing room, between shows," she says.

Her own tastes in music vary. "But I mostly like people like Andy Williams, Stevie Wonder, Dionne Warwick and Clifford T. Ward."

Her one big ambition now is to break into America. She's been there, but only briefly. "I'd really love to have a big hit in the States, and then go over and work there," says Livvy.

Lynsey de Paul, considered by many menfolk to be the dishiest little doll of them all, is now renowned for her ability as a songwriter as well as a singer.

Her voice, she admits, is not the best in the world. But she does know how to put a number over, once she's written a good 'un.

Less than three years in the business, she can already look back on a string of hit records, which include "Sugar Me", the biggie which first launched her, "Getting a Drag" and "Won't Somebody Dance With Me?"

touring America with SLADE
By M.G. Wood

Travelling through America with Slade on a tour is like being a camp follower with an army.

They come, they see, they conquer – and move on, leaving yet another town or city victim to Slade-mania.

Not that the Wolverhampton group, Noddy Holder, Dave Hill, Jim Lea and Don Powell, are as big yet in America as they are back in Britain, where nearly every single they issue goes automatically to the top of the charts.

As Dave Hill points out: "America is so vast. Every state is like a separate country in itself, and there is no single nationwide television pop show – like Top of the Pops – where you can make just one appearance, and next day everybody has heard of you from Land's End to John o' Groats. Here you have to take on each state, one at a time, and win the audiences over. And we'll keep coming back until we've conquered the lot."

And no doubt they will. For their determination, enthusiasm and energy leaves the onlooker quite breathless.

For one thing I learned on the trip was that a pop star's life is far from being an easy one.

The tour took in gigs in Detroit, towns in Kentucky, Missouri, Tennessee and Indiana, and New York, followed by a couple of concerts on the west coast and some recording sessions. The boys were hoping to have at least one day off while in the States so they could go to Disneyland. But it was a concert every night.

The pace even on a short tour was gruelling. But then, it's with these extensive tours of Britain, Europe, Australia and America that the Slade boys work so hard at staying at the top.

The daily routine on their U.S. tour went something like this:

Rise about 11 a.m. or 12 noon, and eat in hotel room.

At one o'clock, be packed and ready to get into the massive limousines to go to the airport.

Hang around the airport until the flight is called, and fly for an hour or two, often through a time change, which is very confusing until you are used to it.

Into a car at the other end, and off to local radio or press interviews. Then back to the hotel to unpack and rest for a while, or watch television in the hotel.

At 7 p.m., be ready once again to get into the cars and go off to

the gig. It may involve several hours of just hanging around before Slade go on stage, if the supporting groups are running late, or equipment is not ready.

About midnight, leave the theatre and return to the hotel. But it's not bedtime yet. Numerous people connected with the gig will be there too and they expect a party.

So it's into someone's room to eat – pizzas two feet in diameter, or a plastic pail the size of a large bucket full of a certain colonel's Kentucky fried chicken – drink, talk and listen to music until three, four or even six in the morning.

And so to bed. The next day, it starts all over again, exactly the same as before.

It is not just gruelling, it is soul-destroying. And it was hardly surprising that occasionally the boys asked their manager, ex-Animal Chas Chandler, if they could drive to the next gig instead of flying, so that at least they would see a little of America other than hotel bedrooms and theatre dressing rooms.

But it is fun as well.

Slade have known each other so long and so well, that they are more like a family than a group. And anyone going along for the ride is immediately made to feel like one of the family.

The nicest thing about Slade is that they really are unspoiled, as basic and down-to-earth as they probably were the first day they left Wolverhampton, totally lacking in pretention.

When they played in Memphis, they were knocked out by the thought that they were in Elvis Presley's hometown. It did not seem to occur to them that in Britain, they're as big as Elvis themselves. And when they found two Slade records in the juke-box of a local club, alongside the wealth of local Memphis talent, they nearly flipped with excitement.

All four share the same sense of humour, and are only too ready to laugh at themselves and at each other. A favourite way of relieving the monotony of a long journey is to reminisce about past disasters in the days when they were still another struggling unknown group.

Luckily they also have the ability to laugh at things that go wrong. For no tour is without its problems, and this one was no exception.

In Memphis, for instance, their sound mixer, Charlie Newnham, a vital member of the group's team, was arrested shortly before Slade were due to go on stage.

His crime? Smoking a cigarette.

The local fire chief had decided to enforce an old, and usually ignored, regulation against smoking in local theatres, and had brought in police reinforcements to help. For some reason the occasion of Slade's concert was chosen to start the clampdown.

Ironically, as we flew into Memphis, Dave Hill had remarked: "This is going to be a great gig, it's our sort of town. The people were really friendly last time we were here."

Instead, we saw hundreds of Slade fans arrested before they had even seen their idols, all for smoking. Plus poor Charlie, innocently working away at his mixing board, cigarette in hand.

The police were most reluctant to do it, mind you. They were enjoying the atmosphere of the occasion just as much as the fans, and one said: "We hate to spoil the kids' enjoyment. But the fire chief has asked for official assistance, so we've got to do it."

Slade were backstage in their reception room – a room set aside for them and their·friends at each gig, inevitably containing a table groaning with food and a fridge full of lager and Coke.

They first knew of the arrest when Chas Chandler went to investigate the long delay in getting Slade's stage equipment ready. He found Charlie in the arms of the law, and the whole show was threatened.

Eventually, he managed to get Charlie off the hook until the end of the show – on a promise of good behaviour!

But as soon as it was all over, he had to be taken away to the police station. And there he spent a couple of hours in the cells, until Chas bailed him out for fifty-five dollars.

Any group more temperamental and less confident than Slade might have been upset by this incident, and their performance on stage could easily have suffered.

But not these fellows. They could hardly stop laughing enough to walk out on to the stage. Jim Lea, noting that the fire chief packed a gun, commented: "Maybe he shoots the fires out." And then the four lads from Wolverhampton went on to give the performance of their lives.

Afterwards, they teased Charlie

– who was still shaking with fear after being locked up with a cell full of rowdy local drunks – far into the night.

There was another near disaster too on this particular trip.

Each night, the massive bank of sound equipment would be packed into a big truck, and driven by a hired Texan driver overnight to the next gig.

Charlie and the "roadies" would travel separately by car. But one day when the truck arrived at the· back door of the theatre in Louisville, Kentucky, the roadies were nowhere in sight. And they had the key to the back of the truck.

The equipment takes several hours to unload and set up on stage, and time was running short. And the padlock on the truck was too formidable to be forced open.

The situation looked tricky, until someone suddenly found the roadies' car at the front of the theatre, its occupants fast asleep.

Arriving a few hours before the truck, they had decided to catch up on a little sleep. And while everyone was pacing anxiously up and down at the back of the theatre, they had been gently snoring away at the other side of the building.

Slade, of course, thought the whole incident hilarious.

Musically, there were problems, too. In two places, Slade shared the bill with a much heavier group called King Crimson, and as Chas Chandler said, "King Crimson and Slade are as different as chalk and cheese, and so are their fans."

We were in Detroit at the time, and he added ominously: "The audiences in Detroit have a reputation for being very hostile if their favourite group are not on stage."

But he need not have worried. Noddy soon had them all on their feet, Slade fans and King Crimson fans alike.

In Indiana, where the same thing happened, the crowd were calling for Slade halfway through the other group's performance.

"They just wanted to rave," said Dave Hill afterwards. "They were shouting 'We want rock and

roll'. It was all quite fantastic."

In Louisville, Kentucky, Slade's competition came from 70,000 Episcopalians, who were holding a religious convention in the town. Slade won hands down – or rather fists, since the Slade symbol of a clenched fist with the thumb up seems now to be a universally adopted badge of identification for all Slade fans.

Well, I bet the Episcopalians didn't get thousands of people on their feet, screaming for more!

With Slade, it's music, music all the way. Even at parties, Dave Hill will be sitting strumming his guitar, working out a new routine.

It's the same backstage before each performance. He and Noddy and Jim will be working out a slightly different introduction to one of their songs, polishing the performance all the time.

At the hotels, the boys would frantically switch the numerous channels on the TV sets, trying to find a pop programme to watch.

And the minute we stepped into the limousines, the boys would reach for the switches. First the radio, and a local music station, and secondly the air conditioning.

It seems odd to speak of Slade as a single unit, as if all four think and act alike all the time. For they are four very individual people. Jim Lea is a joker, full of

boyish charm. He is probably the most gifted, musically, too, and writes the music for many of their songs. A keyboard player as well as a guitarist, he has that habit which so many pianists have – he just cannot pass a piano without rushing over to play a few notes, or work out a new melody which has been going around in his head.

Dave Hill – known as "H" to the others, and "Superyob" to himself – is the spokesman, the businessman, the diplomat and the chatterbox. He never stops talking. But however much he is joking and fooling around, the welfare of Slade is always uppermost in his mind.

He manages to combine business with pleasure, for if any girls turn up at the hotel hoping to see the group, they can always rely on Dave going to talk to them.

He will ask them about themselves, whether they can get Slade records easily at their local shops (if not, the distribution is slipping up somewhere and he will look into it), whether they are going to the concert that night. If they haven't been able to get tickets, he will make sure they get in – somehow. Result? A fan more devoted than ever before.

"Each individual fan means a lot to us," Dave explains. "We want them to get to know us, realise we are just ordinary blokes. I don't want them to be afraid of us, think we're aloof."

His stage outfits get more outrageous all the time. Goodness knows how he was managing to stand up on the platform boots he was sporting in America, never mind strut about the stage the way he does.

Noddy Holder is an enigma, quiet and self-contained off stage, with a wry sense of humour on the rare occasions he says something. But the minute he walks on to that stage he undergoes a whole change of personality.

You can see it happening even backstage, before the performance. His head, normally held oddly to one side like a little boy,

16

continued on page 25

Jimmy Savile

Noel Edmonds

Tony Blackburn

Nazareth

Status Quo

David Essex

Gilbert O'Sullivan

David Cassidy

is suddenly thrown back and he gives out a great yell of exuberance.

As he walks on to the stage, he suddenly acquires a great authority, a stage presence, which can silence 10,000 screaming youngsters. As he kneels on stage, swivelling his head to flash reflections from the mirrors on his famous topper, there is joy in his sparkling eyes, delight in his extraordinary voice.

And afterwards, the adrenalin still surging through him, he can't stop laughing and talking. He will tell funny stories until five in the morning, till people are holding their sides in humorous pain. The next morning, he is quiet little Noddy again.

Don Powell was taking things easy this trip. Going to bed earlier than the others, drinking nothing but soft drinks.

But his performance on the drums was as frenetic as ever, and it was difficult to believe that not so very long before, he had been lying unconscious in hospital after a terrible car crash.

The only sign – apart from his early nights and abstinence – was the plaster which covered his hands. The skin was still too soft for the drum sticks after his weeks in hospital.

He cannot remember anything at all about that crash to this day. In fact, one of his earliest memories, he told me, was waking up and seeing the other three members of the group sitting at the foot of his bed with worried faces.

"I thought I was at home, and wondered what on earth the lads were doing there," he said. "When we started rehearsing for the tour, it was frightening, really weird. I couldn't remember any of our numbers. Nod would say 'Let's do "Cum on Feel The Noize"' and I wouldn't be able to remember the introduction.

"But gradually it all came back to me. The others never made a fuss of me, or treated me like an invalid, but just acted naturally with me, and I'm sure that is what helped me to get better so quickly. The doctor told me that the best cure would just be to get back to work, and be with the lads again. And he was right."

Another member of the Slade "family" is Graham Swinnerton, known as Swin, their chief roadie and tour manager. His job is to get Slade to wherever they are meant to be, to organise travel, get tickets, make sure everyone is in the right room and has everything he wants. He is like a nanny, mother, accountant and

bodyguard all rolled into one.

On long journeys, when everyone else was dozing, you would suddenly hear this quiet little tapping sound. It was Swin, totting up the hotel bills with the aid of his little pocket-sized electronic calculator. Not until the gig is safely over, and everybody back at the hotel, does Swin relax and enjoy himself for the first time in the day.

I left them in St. Louis, winning over yet another new audience, notching up another conquest on the Slade belt.

"The first time we came to America," said Jim Lea, "we were totally unknown, just a twenty-minute act at the bottom of the bill, sort of introducing ourselves. Then, the second time, we were beginning to get popular and worked our way up to the top of the bill by the end of the tour.

"This time, it's great, and we're having a marvellous reception. But on one date, in a town where we're not known at all, we shall be the supporting group again. You see, we just have to go out there and prove ourselves all over again, and maybe by the end of the evening, we'll have won over seventy per cent of the audience as new Slade fans. We just hope so, anyway."

touring SLADE

OSMOND

When you follow a group around like the Osmonds, you get used to noise. You have to. Because life is pretty hectic for the six lads from the United States of America. And when they come to Britain to do a concert tour, well, there's only one word to describe it . . . that's OSMOND-mania!

Not since the far-off days of the Beatles have we witnessed such amazing screamage scenes.

By now, the Osmond brothers – and Mum and Dad, and sister Marie, too, I guess – have all learned to live with noise. Permanent noise. The noise of little girls screaming at their concerts. Screeching outside their hotel windows. And shrieking hysterically whenever the boys have the nerve to set foot outside.

Such was the fervour of the fans for the Osmonds – and for David Cassidy, too – when they were in London that it became impossible for the BBC to actually invite them to the studio to appear on Top of the Pops.

Instead, they had to be filmed, away from London . . . because the programme chiefs at the BBC were genuinely afraid there might be an accident of some sort with so many thousands of girls milling around the TV studios on a busy main road, in the hope of catching a glimpse of their American idols.

So you can guess what it was like being on tour with a group like the Osmonds. . . .

It's a Sunday . . . the boys fly in from America. In a private jet, with the name OSMONDS emblazoned across the plane.

Even at the airport, the pandemonium is unbelievable. Thousands of girls have been waiting for hours, many of them all night . . . perched precariously on the observation roof at Heathrow.

The boys arrive, wave at the fans from the tarmac for a few minutes, and are then whisked away in giant limousines . . . to their London hotel, which is being kept a strict secret.

No red carpet welcome, however. The boys are smuggled

quietly into the rear entrance . . . usually used strictly by tradesmen and delivery vans.

They are shown to their various rooms. A big family, so there are a lot of suitcases. Are they hungry? Yes, they answer, pretty well in unison. Would they like a snack to keep them going until dinner? Yes, please! What's it to be? The order goes out from the Osmond kids: "Seven steak sandwiches and seven bottles of the soft drink Seven Up."

Now they are virtually prisoners in their own hotel, because within a few hours, it has leaked out. Their hiding-place has been found by the fans. The hotel is soon surrounded. And the hotel has had to put men on all doors, to stop Osmond fans from getting inside.

While the boys whittle away their time, strumming guitars, watching television, just talking – or little Jimmy, the baby of the group, playing with his toys, a model car and a new football – the men who operate the well-oiled Osmond machine go into action in another part of the hotel.

There are meetings between their manager, their record company publicist, their producer and the man responsible for the boys' safety and security while they are in this country.

Strong-arm bodyguards are scattered around at various points in the hotel . . . employed just to keep out the girls, who are now prepared to undergo a round-the-clock vigil. They squat down for the night outside the hotel, and it takes several kindly policemen to assure them that there is no point in staying as the boys will not be coming out tonight.

Some of the girls drift off home, weeping. Others stay . . . just in case they can catch a glimpse. A face at a window would do!

Next day, it's off to Manchester. Another flight. . . . More girls at the airport. More screams. More struggles to see the six most popular lads in the world. More tears, as some girls miss the sight of their idols.

At the King's Hall, where the concert is being staged, girls have paid up to £2 for a ticket to see the Osmonds. But money doesn't matter, they tell you. They just want to see the boys in action. And if possible get up on stage and grab a handful of any one of them. Donny, preferably.

Meanwhile, gifts start to pour in for the boys. Scarves, ties, knitted sweaters. And cards and letters – hundreds of them – some with long poems talking of undying love.

Some of the letters actually do get through to the boys. Donny reads some of the cards, and smiles gently. The smile of a teenager who knows just what it's like to have a thousand girls all in love with you at the same time.

Donny and Marie Osmond

teenagers. Their ages vary, but mostly the girls range from ten and eleven to fifteen and sixteen.

Inside the theatre. The show is on – at last. The audience – mostly girls, but some boys here and there, and a few Mums too – is pent up with excitement. The lights go out. Total darkness. The boys are ushered up quietly on to the stage. They enter the arena, like handsome young gladiators going out to face the lions.

Suddenly, the music strikes up. The lights come on... blue, yellow, red and green.... As the six white-suited fellers are caught in the flashing lights, an absolute crescendo of screams rises from the packed, jubilant audience.

The boys go into their musical routine. They're fast and furious. And very professional. They wiggle their bottoms in unison, leap in the air, shuffle and prance around the stage, playing those guitars for all they are worth.

Donny goes to the piano, falls back on his stool and plays it with one hand.... The girls in the front rows of seats surge forward in one wild, enthusiastic mass.

The strong-arm men surrounding the stage join arms to add strength to their ranks. They push back the tide of little girls, now fighting and kicking and flailing their arms in an effort to get on to the stage. Some girls do actually manage to get as far as the stage, before being lifted bodily off and carried away. Others, poor things, are simply in tears, quivering in their seats. But their tears are tears of ecstacy. All their pent-up emotions come flooding out. They have no inhibitions left.

Finally, the show is over.... The boys have played themselves silly. They are hoarse. And wet through with perspiration. A van is waiting for them at the back of the theatre.

There's no time to change, the boys know that. Hurriedly, they are each given a massive blanket and a towel, and bundled un-ceremoniously into the back of the van. "Come on, boys," some-one shouts. "Let them get to the plane. They're still soaking."

On the night of the concert ... the boys look slightly edgy and anxious. They are a little nervous, but energetic and ready to go. They discuss together just how they're going to "rip 'em up" tonight.

Outside, the first batch of girls, anxiously clutching their tickets, set up a chant: "We want the Osmonds...We want the Osmonds ... We want the Osmonds." They are relentless in their war cry, and their shouts are accompanied menacingly by a fierce banging of fists on the theatre doors.

The police are worried. One or two girls have already fainted in the crush, even before the doors have been opened, and a feeling of hysteria is building up among the ranks of quivering youngish

And it's off on the plane again. This time to Glasgow. Another day. But the same scenes. Another concert. More snatched meals for the hardworking men who surround the boys day and night. Ambulances at the ready at every concert, waiting to whisk away the injured or take care of the hysterically uncontrollable young girls who find it all too much. Fortunately, most of the girls who faint are suffering from nervous tension, and they soon recover and are back on their feet again, to exercise their lungs with a fresh outburst of screaming.

Back at the hotel. Now in London. In the corridor outside the rooms of the Osmond family, one of the tough security men is tucking quietly into a sandwich and a bottle of beer. He says, "They really are the closest family I've ever come across. And genuinely nice with it. But it's a tremendous responsibility looking after their safety."

Off stage, the Osmonds are, truly, a quite remarkable family. They seem to do everything together. They are devoutly religious, and it's not just a gimmick.

Their mother says, quite unashamedly, "All our family is Christian. I think in most people there is a desire for goodness and hopefulness, and my boys have tried to keep this kind of good image. They do have a responsibility and a leadership, and I know the boys don't want to let any of those kids down.

"In this respect, I think they are very good missionaries for the Christian religion. The church is very happy with what they're doing. Right now, they're probably accomplishing as much as if they were all full-time missionaries."

And the boys all go along with this, too. Said Wayne: "The Mormon faith, which we follow, is very important to all of us. It's the reason why we all started. We actually got started by singing in our church, and from there it moved on to bigger things."

Alan, who tends to be the spokesman for the group, says: "We feel we have the answer to everything, because we stick to the Christian faith. Money is not that important to us. Of course we don't dismiss money altogether. We know that we have good guidance as to investments. So long as we have enough money to get plenty to eat and plenty to wear, that's all we really worry about."

The trip doesn't last long, before they're off again. This time, waving goodbye at Heathrow Airport to the thousands more devoted Osmond worshippers. Off to the Continent. For more concerts. More screams at the airport. More police protection. More noise.

And then back to America. Really, the only time the Osmonds can be assured of peace and quiet is when they're back home in their hillside ranch in Utah.

The Osmonds. In action on stage. Enough Teen appeal to set 10,000 girls screaming

IT AIN'T SO EASY...

Ex-actor Robin Nash is a very different kind of guy from Johnnie Stewart, the producer who first launched Top of the Pops and has been the backbone of the programme ever since.

But one thing they both have in common is a love and a fascination for pop music.

Robin, who has temporarily taken over from Johnnie for his longest-ever stint as producer of TV's top-rating pop show, is a producer with a very varied background. He's done everything — from drama and comedy . . . to children's programmes. And he is equally at home with any of them, he says.

For several years, he produced "Dixon of Dock Green". Then he was involved in an assortment of TV comedy shows — such as "Marriage Lines" and "Meet The Wife".

Since then, he's been responsible for producing programmes ranging from "Burke's Special" to "Basil Brush" and "Crackerjack".

But Top of the Pops. he says, keeps him on his toes — because it's such a snappy, lively programme which demands quick decisions, as well as a good deal of behind-the-scenes plotting and planning.

"Musically, my own tastes vary — from Wagner, at one end of the scale, to Pink Floyd and the Sweet at the other," says Robin. "I adore the natural amusement brought into the pop field by artists like Gary Glitter, and I happen to admire artists like Leo Sayer for the thought and planning that goes into a record.

"I'm inclined to look at the whole business very dispassionately when it comes to producing the programme. I've got to be very commercial. I'm really only interested in putting into Top of the Pops the kind of artists I think the viewers at home would like to see."

The programme largely makes itself, of course, because the format is still — as it always has been — based purely on the best-selling records in the single pop charts.

"We simply mirror what is in the charts. But isn't that why the programme is so successful?" asks Robin.

"The charts reflect what people are buying in the record shops. Our job is to give it to them via TV. To me, this is the all-important thing in my job as the producer of such a show."

The problems? There are several, he admits.

"Our main aim is to have for the viewing public the most successful groups and singers as quickly as I can possibly get them on the screen."

Producer Robin Nash, discussing an item in the show with Cliff Richard

Most of the leading singers and groups are queueing up, of course, to appear on the show. After all, Top of the Pops gives the best possible TV exposure any artist could ever wish for. "But I am limited, some weeks, in the artists I can actually get on to the programme," says Robin.

"For a start, there is often a problem in getting American artists, simply because they are not readily available."

But he has very definite views on this, anyway. "I'm extremely patriotic," Robin emphasises. "It is, after all, a British show, so I try to get as many British artists on as I possibly can. I do tend to 'think British'.

"If it's a straight choice, I'll always put a British group in before someone from overseas. I happen to like the British product best."

He does not like, too often, having to play a number and not having the artist or group on the show to perform it.

"I much prefer to have the artists in the studio, performing 'live' whenever possible, so that the kids in the audience can see them. This creates more atmosphere."

But he does, nevertheless, try to build up a stock of what he calls "outside walkabout" film material of various big-name artists — and this is screened when the artists themselves just cannot be available to appear in person on the programme.

The BBC production team receives all the new record releases — some sixty or seventy discs — every week. They all have to be played and listened to — sometimes three or four times.

"It's not always easy to pick out a good record on the first play," says Robin. "Often, a record doesn't strike you as anything different until you've heard it two or three times."

The programme's "Tip for the Top" record each week is invariably chosen from the top thirty to fifty records in the chart.

The practice is only to have artists on with records that are going up in the charts; never those that are going down.

"My one big nightmare," laughs Robin, "is that one week a record will jump into the charts, straight to No. 1, and everything else will move down one place in the Top Thirty. So with every other record going down, I'll be left with only one new hit number to play!"

He now wakes up in the morning, he says, to a radio alarm clock . . . so he starts every day listening to pop music. He also has the radio on in his car whenever he's driving.

The satisfaction of the job of being producer? "Suddenly discovering a brand-new artist," says Robin, without hesitation. "It gives me a great personal kick to find a singer with something completely new to offer, and then see him make the pop charts and go on to much bigger things.

"I remember this was the case with Peter Skellern. I woke up one morning, and was in the bathroom, shaving, at seven o'clock, when I heard this fellow on the radio, singing 'You're A Lady'.

"When I got into my office, I told my secretary to find out who this chap was because I wanted him for Top of the Pops. She kept interrupting me by telling me about some new artist. I said 'I don't care. Just find out who this fellow was on the record I heard this morning.'

"She came back later in the day and said, 'That's who I was trying to tell you about — Peter Skellern. That's the fellow you heard on the radio.'

"I think everyone thought I was a bit mad when I first put him on the show. But I liked him."

The same for Leo Sayer, another artist Robin Nash helped to "push". "I thought this fellow had a very different 'sound' and he'd obviously worked hard at it. I wanted to promote his first record, but it was a case of there being too many important record releases at that time.

"But I found Leo Sayer's sound was 'arresting'. It struck me as being very different from the run-of-the-mill pop stuff. So I put him on with his second record . . . and he became very successful."

ROY WOOD

It was Roy Wood who brought the magic back into pop. More than any other musician, Roy Wood came up with a much-needed touch of magic when he quit his old group, the Electric Light Orchestra, and formed Wizzard.

Since then, Roy, a shy young man from Birmingham who hides behind his war paint, has gone from strength to strength in the music world.

Weird, he may have looked – with his forest of hair, dyed an assortment of gay colours, green, red, blue, yellow, purple. He made up with strange, black-magic symbols daubed on his face.

But every pop artist needs a gimmick of some sort to break through ▶

to the big time. And this was simply Roy's eccentric way of announcing boldly: "I've arrived!"

Wood – and the musicians who back him – have always provided fun. There's been nothing nasty in their make-up or in their brand of music.

Their performances on Top of the Pops over the last year or two have been hilarious, as well as musically entertaining. They've been self-mocking, too – with the guys in the band sporting outrageous DA hairstyles and pointing their saxophones to the sky with gay abandon. It all summed up the frivolous excitement and natural love that both Roy and the rest of the boys feel for good old-fashioned rock 'n' roll.

A year or so ago, Elvis Presley called Roy Wood over to America – to help him recapture some of that pop magic which, obviously, the American King of Rock must have felt he'd lost over the years.

Roy was only too happy to help out. With a talent like his, he can afford to be generous!

Wood is an amazing little man. He is shy to the point of embarrassment – which might explain his freakish, extrovert behaviour on stage, whether he's whooping it up with Wizzard, or just being plain Roy Wood, at the piano.

He is no newcomer to the pop scene, of course. He's been around

the music scene since the mid-sixties and he has a musical talent which is really quite unique.

Born in Birmingham – 8th November 1946 – he was expelled from art school . . . and so turned to music. He taught himself to play every musical instrument he could lay his hands on . . . guitar, saxophone, cello, oboe, bassoon, tuba, French horn, clarinet, banjo, sitar, harmonica, string bass, and even drums.

Wood is, in fact, a one-man orchestra. For he can play every instrument in the band. Which isn't bad for a bloke who had no formal musical training!

On his first solo album, "Boulders", which was hailed as something of a pop masterpiece, Roy proved his musical talent – by playing every instrument himself, writing all the songs, and producing the record, complete with lead and backing vocal tracks.

Yet he can't read music. He has his own system of writing music, he explains, based on letters of the alphabet. "The composer who has influenced me most is Tchaikovsky. No one ever wrote better melodies than he did," says Roy. "And even with a frenzied rock 'n' roll beat, melody is still what it's all about."

Roy has always been a musical wanderer. An innovator. He is a restless sort of character, never

34

staying in the same place too long. Always seeking out fresh musical pastures. And anxious to experiment with new rhythms and new ideas.

It's been the same with his bands. He started out playing with various groups around Birmingham. First it was with Mike Sheridan and the Nightriders. Then came the formation of The Move. This was the group who smashed up TV sets, let off fireworks, chopped up effigies of Adolf Hitler on stage, and scored several big hits – long before Alice Cooper was heard of in America.

Then Roy grew restless. So he quit The Move and formed the Electric Light Orchestra, with a few rock 'n' roll buddies and one or two renegades from the London Symphony Orchestra.

This was the band which really rocked the pop world, because they derived a new pop sound – rock with classical connotations.

But then again, Roy wanted something new. He left the ELO and immediately formed Wizzard. From their very first disc, "Ball Park Incident", the new group was a hit.

The Move, Electric Light Orchestra, Wizzard . . . whichever band he's worked with, Roy Wood has steered them all to a distinctively different sound.

Some of his songs will never be forgotten. Songs like "I Can Hear The Grass Grow", "Flowers In The Rain" and "Brontosaurus" have all become rock classics.

As a melody writer, he is on a par with Paul McCartney. He's written some gorgeous melodies and some absorbing lyrics, all mixed up with a high degree of humour when the occasion calls for it.

Roy makes no secret of the fact that he plays music simply to entertain. "People now want more than somebody stood up there on stage playing in their jeans," he says. "Showbiz is back, and I'm glad."

Who would dare to deny that Mr. Wood has done his share to bring about such a happy situation?

I RECOGNISE THAT FACE!

Here's a Top Ten to really set you guessing. . . .

Ten pictures of some of the faces who made it big in the music world. And they all appeared on Top of the Pops at some time over the last eleven years.

Some of them, of course, are no longer around. The groups have disbanded, and gone their separate ways.

But some of the artists are still very much with us. Though they've changed somewhat in appearance.

Can you spot them? It might be helpful to have Mum or Dad around on this one.

One point for each group you successfully recognise. And another point if you can remember a big hit record they produced.

(Answers on page 77)

3

6

10

the backers

by Norma Matheson

PAN'S PEOPLE

Pan's People are as much a part of Top of the Pops as the DJs who present the shows and the pop groups themselves. It is difficult to remember a time when they weren't dancing on the programme. In fact it is seven years since they started dancing regularly on the show.

The group started in 1966 when six girls, already all impressive dancers, joined together. The original line-up in those days was Flick Colby (who now does the choreography for the group), Ruth Pearson, Babs Lord, Dee Dee Wilde, Louise Clarke and Andy Rutherford. But Andy (real name Andrea) left to have a baby a couple of years ago, and she was replaced by Cherry Gillespie.

Before coming to Top of the Pops, they had worked on a TV series in Amsterdam and also done a couple of TV shows in Britain. But it was Colin Charman who gave the group their first real break with an appearance on Top of the Pops. And they have never looked back.

The Pan's girls usually have two or three days to learn a routine, and Flick Colby takes a day to choreograph it. "But it's getting faster every week," she tells you. "It's amazing just what you can do under pressure."

Flick decides, with the director of the programme, which record Pan's People will dance to. Usually, they try to give Flick a choice, but the record has to come from the Top Thirty.

"I try and get as much variety as possible into our dancing," Flick explains. "Dancers get bored doing the same things over and over again."

How has the dancing changed over the years since they started on the show? "A lot," says Flick. "Especially in the clothes the girls wear. And because the clothes have changed, the dancing has changed too. There were certain things the dancers could do in a mini skirt that they just couldn't do in a long dress. And you can do things flailing a long dress which would look ridiculous in a mini skirt.

Every week, Pan's People have to appear in a different set of costumes, and these are made for the girls after Flick has decided what record they will dance to, and how they will tackle it. Then she tries to find a costume which will suit the music.

"We get quite a lot of letters from people who want to borrow the costumes, or asking where they can buy them," says Ruth.

They get a lot of fanmail. "We get lots of letters from the Forces," says Dee Dee. "And from little girls who enjoy the dresses we wear. A lot of people also ask us to write down the dances we do — just as if you can stick a dance in an envelope!"

Ruth tells me: "There are a couple of girls who formed their own group and they usually pick the same record as us, then do their own version of a dance routine and come down and show us."

Pan's People have all had formal dance training and were unanimous about always having wanted to become dancers. So what advice, I wondered, would they give to young girls who wanted to become professional dancers?

Firstly, it seems, you must start early in life and you must be prepared to do a lot of hard work. Flick emphasises the importance of self discipline and says that if you really work hard, you can get somewhere. Ruth says that she felt too many people seem to think of it as a terribly glamorous job, and although it does have its moments — maybe a couple of hours one day a week — I would hardly call rehearsing in an empty rugby club glamorous!

The other thing to bear in mind is that a dancer's career is a relatively short one, and there is always a great deal of competition for jobs. "Obviously, you go on dancing for as long as you can," says Louise. "Some people have still been dancing when they're thirty-five."

But what happens to them after they give up dancing? "You don't have to go into complete retirement," says Cherry, who is the baby of the group. "You can, of course, try and carry on as a choreographer, or maybe start to teach dancing to younger girls."

PAN'S PEOPLE LINE-UP
Dee Wilde was born Patricia Wilde in Farnham, Surrey. From the age of three until she was seventeen, she lived in West Africa. Before joining Pan's People she was with a small group of dancers, and toured Spain.

Ruth Pearson was born in Kingston, Surrey, and started dancing at the age of seven. When she was thirteen, she was awarded a grant from Surrey County Council to the Ballet Rambert. At seventeen, she left to attend the Corona Stage School, and she taught at LAMDA while still only seventeen.

Barbara (Babs) Lord was born in Wolverhampton. She started dancing at the age of three in her mother's stage school. She later spent six years at the Arts Educational Trust stage school.

Louise Clarke comes from London, and started dancing when she was four. At eleven, she went to the Corona Stage School and while she was there did a lot of child modelling, TV and film work.

Cherry Gillespie was born in Hemsby, near Great Yarmouth. She started dancing when she was four. At thirteen she went to an adult dancing school, having accomplished ballet at a junior school. And she joined Pan's People straight from dancing school.

THE LADYBIRDS. . .

The Ladybirds have been putting in the vocal "lah-lah-lah's" since Top of the Pops first moved to the London studios, from Manchester, over eight years ago. The group of singers backing a solo singer are often forgotten and are rarely seen on the screen. But without them there would be no choruses, no "lah-de-dah's".

The three girls started singing just over ten years ago as a result of a meeting between Maggie Stredder and Gloria George. At that time, both were already singers, although Maggie was working for a spell with Lionel Blair. They had no idea just what starting a group would entail, but they both thought it was a novel plan.

Their name, The Ladybirds, came from their first record — the nursery rhyme "Ladybird, ladybird fly away home". There is now another group called The Ladybirds on the Continent. "They are a Danish group who work absolutely starkers," Maggie told me with a chuckle.

As the usual backing group needs to have three people in the line-up, Maggie and Gloria had to look for a third girl to join them. They found a third singer, but she was later replaced by Marian Davies, who has been with the group now for seven years.

They remained unchanged from the time of Marian joining the group until last February when Gloria left. She gave up the music business completely to go and run a motel in Miami.

When they first started on Top of the Pops, of course, it was the era of the solo singer. "In one show we would be doing three or four songs, backing people like Tom Jones, Engelbert and Cilla," Marian explained. "But now, with more groups being so popular, we don't have nearly as much vocal backing to do."

Besides Top of the Pops, the group do a lot of recording sessions and other television work.

"Although we get a lot of work, there is fierce competition in this business. There never seems to be a shortage of people who want to become singers, and I've known some very talented people who just never get work."

On advice to any would-be singers, Maggie says: "The main thing is that they learn to read music. This is absolutely essential. We don't learn, we don't have time to, the songs that we sing on the programme. We simply read the songs straight off.

"Apart from that, people shouldn't think of it as a stepping-stone to stardom. It has been known for a backing singer or session musician to become a star, but it is not very often that this happens. People who sing in backing groups do it because that is what they want to do.

The Ladybirds are certainly one vocal group who are perfectly happy and contented to stay in the background.

JOHNNY PEARSON

Hidden away in the corner of the Top of the Pops studio is the orchestra, with its musical director and pianist Johnny Pearson.

Johnny has been directing the TOP orchestra since it was first introduced on the programme. "The need for an orchestra came about because of the law introduced by the Musicians' Union regarding miming, tracking, dubbing on television," says Johnny. "So in order for the programme to continue, it was necessary to have a full orchestra. And Johnnie Stewart, who was then producing the show, asked me if I'd form one and be the musical director.

"Solo singers, of course, need the full orchestral backing. Whereas the groups provide all their own accompaniment."

The orchestra is made up of top session musicians, though they are not tied down to doing only Top of the Pops every week.

Johnny says he has seen a lot of changes, not only with the music, since he started doing the TV show, but also in the outlook in production, which is very important if a programme is to remain a popular one.

Since colour was introduced, there have been some revolutionary changes.

"This makes things highly complex, and all sorts of little snags have to be overcome before each week's programme. The show is run on a very tight schedule. Quite often we won't know what numbers are going to be in the programme only hours before it goes on the air, and this is something I don't think people appreciate at all."

The orchestra not only has to be rehearsed, but a sound balance reached and made perfect for recording. "Besides this, I have to liaise with the artists we will be providing the accompaniment for, and make sure they are quite happy with what we are doing," says Johnny.

"When there are a lot of groups high in the pop charts, we don't have so many musical items to do, as a band. But this situation often changes quite dramatically, and there's a sudden revival of the solo artists. That's when we are suddenly busy again."

Johnny Pearson has had success himself in the recording field, of course. With Sounds Orchestral, he had a big hit with "Cast Your Fate To The Winds" some years back. And more recently, he was back in the charts with "Sleepy Shores", the theme music for the BBC TV series "Owen, MD" — another mammoth hit.

Johnny's background in music is a classical one. He started playing piano at the age of seven and after studying at the London Academy of Music and Dramatic Art for six years, he studied with Solomon, the world-famous concert pianist and great exponent of Beethoven.

How does he feel now, not being seen so often, and conducting the orchestra from behind a screen? "Well, of course it is lovely to be seen, but it's really not practical to have a whole orchestra in full vision," he says. "An orchestra takes up a lot of room and it's much more difficult to get a proper balance of instruments in a big studio. Besides, a programme like Top of the Pops is essentially for the groups and the singers."

Johnny's advice to young people who want to become musicians is this: "Put in a lot of practice. You must be well taught and have a good solid background to whatever instrument you choose to play. It's not easy to become a professional musician — you'll soon find out if you're good enough to get anywhere. There is a lot of competition, but this is a good thing.

"For the professional musician, there are a lot of pitfalls, heartaches and a lot of jolly hard work. You have some good times and some tremendous happenings that make you feel wonderful and that it is all worth it.

But you have to pay for those moments. The strain of performing in front of an audience is great. Once you are out there you have to overcome nerves. This is something some people never manage to do successfully, and so they never perform at their best."

Does he still get nervous before a performance? "Oh yes — every time," he says.

Donny Osmond

Mud

Gary Glitter

Roy Wood

David Bowie

Slade

The Carpenters

ROCK 'N' ROLL

IT'S STILL ALIVE AND KICKING

by Gavin Petrie

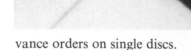

What is supposed to have died at the end of the 1950's but has been resurrected yearly ever since? Why, rock 'n' roll, of course!

And it is even more evident this year, with the idols of today searching for the same mood and glamour that they were spellbound by in their youth. Can you imagine young Gary Glitter or young Marc Bolan at the front of the stage reaching out to touch their idols? Well, you can bet they did!

Marc Bolan came in touch with rock 'n' roll virtually by accident. Young Marc was particularly enamoured with the theme tune from a film about an early American frontiersman called Davy Crockett, which was sung by Bill Hayes. So Marc's father went out to buy him the record, but came back with a record by Bill Haley, the man who started rock 'n' roll.

He confesses he was bitterly disappointed – until he heard the record. "Then I rocked – and I've been rocking ever since."

In fact, Marc was around the music business for some time, in and out of various rock 'n' roll bands, but, like David Bowie, abandoned it to perform his wildly poetic songs with the aid of an acoustic guitar. As part of the duo Tyrannosaurus Rex, he was wildly acclaimed in the Flower Power days.

But it was he who returned to the electric guitar and undoubtedly started the glam rock movement in the dark days of 1970. He sparked off a new cult with "Hot Love" and "Ride A White Swan".

He brightened up a lot of people's lives to the extent of having sold millions and millions of records. At one time, he even had something like 400,000 ad-

vance orders on single discs.

Then suddenly, after four years of criticism and leading the glam rock movement, he cut his curls and removed the make-up, saying, "I believe it is all a thing of the past."

But if he is disillusioned by glamour, one man who certainly is not is **Gary Glitter**. He made his first record as Paul Gadd, from Banbury, when he was only fourteen – a ditty called "Alone In The Night". Then he changed his name to Paul Raven – making nine records under that name.

He is no newcomer to television pop. As Paul Raven, he used to be the man who "warmed up" the audiences for the well-known ITV pop show "Ready Steady, Go!", which was at one time a deadly rival to Top of the Pops.

When he finally broke through with the massive hit "Rock 'n' Roll Parts 1 and 2" he loved all the glamour that goes with it.

Gary Glitter

And he loves talking, too. Gary's publicist once arranged a series of interviews – twenty minutes to each journalist. By the time the schedule was three hours behind, she had to drag the journalists out when their time had elapsed – with Gary Glitter still talking, nonstop.

I recall Gary telling me, "At first nobody took me seriously. Then people started to get into what I was doing."

So much so that one big-name star I know went along to see Gary's show just to criticise it, but afterwards confessed to Gary that he couldn't knock it "because it was the best thing I've ever seen."

"The thing is," says Gary, "people mustn't get carried away with the musical aspect too much. What we do is make great pop records.

"We wanted to put some fun into the music. I think music has been getting too serious. Rock 'n' roll is fun. Kids want to get up and stamp around.

"Those early rock 'n' roll songs have influenced our writing (he writes with his manager, Mike Leander). There were dozens of rock 'n' roll songs that sounded similar but yet were quite different."

Now, **Alvin Stardust** didn't only dream of being a rock 'n' roll star – he *was* a rock 'n' roller from way back.

Like Gary Glitter, he had a previous stage name – Shane Fenton. He wore gold lamé suits and fronted a band called the Fentones who were very successful in the early Sixties. It has been about ten years since he quit the singing side of the business, when he was really on the crest of a wave.

He then became part of a successful management agency, handling people like Lulu. But his interest in office work declined and he decided to travel the world, finally arriving back in Britain from New York, penniless.

He tried a spell doing cabaret, telling jokes and singing songs. But as he said later, "It drove me nearly mad."

That's when he remembered rock 'n' roll, bought a guitar, and went out on the road just singing rock, pure and simple.

Then he got together with his manager, recorded some songs, and the lad from Knotty Ash with the Liverpudlian twang became Alvin Stardust. He burst back on the scene, as big as ever, last year with "Coo Ca Choo" which shot up the charts and put the experienced Mr. Stardust back in the big time.

His first TV appearance on a children's show was calculated to attract attention – which it did. Alvin was all fluffy hair, and pinks and blue. Still no one recognised him until he appeared on Top of the Pops when, once he had donned his rocker's black leather gear, the secret was out!

A man whom you wouldn't recognise without his make-up is that classic rocker **Roy Wood**. Now here is a man who has every right to be confident that his songs will be hits.

In his ten years in rock 'n' roll, only his first band, the Nightriders, did not have a hit record. His second band, the Move, formed in 1965, The Electric Light Orchestra and Wizzard, both formed in the Seventies, have all had massive hits. In fact, records by the Move are now something of a special cult in America.

Roy has come round to rock 'n' roll again through Wizzard. Although he tends to take the mickey out of the Glory of the Fifties, his singles are treated seriously and hailed as classics.

In the field of bizarre make-up and glamour, Roy is not just copying the fashion – his bands have always had gimmicks. Even with his first band, the Nightriders, he used to impersonate Dusty Springfield, complete with blonde wig and make-up.

"What I'm trying to do," says Roy, "is mix the sounds into a fusion that people can accept. The time has come when audiences need to be entertained. They need something to look at, which is why basically we make fools of ourselves up on stage."

Suzi Quatro

David Bowie

50

like David Cassidy, but when everyone thought he was going to be Britain's answer to Cassidy and Donny Osmond, there he was – the first David Essex with an aggressive rock song!

Aggressiveness is something that **Suzi Quatro** worries about. I first met Suzi just after she arrived in Britain. She was wearing patched jeans, had frizzy hair and was carrying a huge bass guitar that she would not let me carry for her. "I've got to learn to carry it around myself," she said.

It's debatable now whether she will have to carry it ever again. Her success since "Can The Can" has been enormous. But her independence, sometimes mistaken for aggressiveness, has remained the same.

"The Detroit tigress", as she is often known, comes from a family of musicians. Her brother Mike has had a couple of hit albums in the States, and one of her sisters, Patti, joined the all-girl group Fanny.

But what of **David Bowie**, the star who, like Bolan, went from a rock 'n' roll band that lived in a van outside London's famous Marquee Club, to the solo artist, then gradually built up again to the great rock 'n' roll band that climaxed with "Ziggy Stardust and the Spiders from Mars"?

The album he released about the time he quit, called "Pin Ups", was his tribute to the best of the London Sixties rock 'n' roll.

His "quitting" the music scene probably turned him into the busiest man around. He is producing two shows – one based on Ziggy Stardust, and the science fantasy novel *1984*. He is much in demand as a session musician (when *Disc* was at his home, Adam Faith phoned up to ask if he would play guitar on his album. David confessed: "I'm not much of a guitarist – are you sure you wouldn't like me to do some saxophone? I'm much better at that").

He's also now producing his own albums, as well as LP's for other artists.

Retired from rock 'n' roll? Some hope!

baby. "I applied for an audition out of desperation," he says now.

Although he found fame acting, he is not an actor-turned-singer. "I've always felt I was a rock singer who was acting."

David's career began nine years ago when he was a drummer with a blues band and later he also became vocalist as well. But the band collapsed, leaving him as a solo artist.

He wasn't even in his teens during the rock 'n' roll heyday of the Fifties. But he, too, liked the directness of rock music.

"At a superficial level," he says, "I like the clothes." He was given all the clothes of the character of Jim MacLaine in the film "That'll Be The Day", and he says this comprises most of his wardrobe. His hairstyle does not owe so much to rock 'n' roll as natural unruliness, which his wife attacks with scissors from time to time.

He surprised everyone by being good-looking and good-natured

What Roy also lacks is sleep. He spends most of his time writing, recording Wizzard, as well as himself, and other bands. So this gives him no more than four hours sleep most nights. What keeps Roy and the Wizzard group organised is his old friend and bass player Rick Price, who gets them all to gigs on time.

But it was no party for **David Essex** to reach the top as a rocker. He came to fame through the stage musical "Godspell", which was his last hope. He was on the dole and his wife was expecting a

TOP DEEJAYS

A few years ago now, a new unknown singer made his debut on the RCA record label. The song on the record was called "Alkatrazz", and the singer was a fellow called Kirk Houston.

That wasn't his real name, however. The real identity of the singer of that one and only record can now be revealed. It was none other than Noel Edmonds, now established as one of the presenters of Top of the Pops.

Noel laughs now at the memory of it. "The record wasn't so much released — it escaped," he quips. "I really had a fancy at that time to be a singer. But not any more. I promise. I've dropped that particular ambition. I now know my limitations."

Not so very long ago, I recall Noel saying, quite emphatically, "I cannot imagine myself as a disc jockey at twenty-five."

Well, he's now twenty-five. In fact, coming up twenty-six.

He laughed when I reminded him of what he'd said. "I know," says Noel. "But really, I still feel I'm not cut out to be a disc jockey for a very long time. I'm much more mature now.

"Over the last year, I've really had to make up my mind about what I want to do — career-wise.

"And I've discovered that I was really enjoying myself much more than I realised. I've now started appreciating how well off I am, compared with lots of people, and the jobs they do. I'm really a lot more fortunate than I thought."

Noel is a very philosophical kind of guy. "I suddenly sat down and started to think things out," he says. "I think maybe I was trying to rush things too much. I was not sitting back and enjoying myself quite as much as I should do. I was thinking too much of the next stepping-stone in the river — and not standing back to look at the pleasant view.

"I really had some very hairy-fairy ideas not so long ago. What I didn't want to be was just another disc jockey. What I didn't then realise — but I do now — is that the best way not to be classed like somebody else is simply to do what they've done, but do it differently.

"Already, I think, I've proved that I'm not just another Tony Blackburn. Tony and I are two completely different personalities, and we both have our quite distinctive characteristics."

Noel, as well as presenting Top of the Pops, is now into all kinds of things, away from the radio and TV studios.

When he's not in the studios, he's busy in

Noel Edmonds

other fields. For instance, he is quite an enterprising young businessman. With a young business partner, Noel owns a couple of record shops — one in London's swinging King's Road, and another in Orpington.

"Pop music is my business," says Noel. "And I think I know by now just what records the kids like to buy, and to hear."

He has strong views, however, on why a lot of people often neglect LP records put out by artists, and concentrate only on buying singles. "There's a whole lot of good material on many albums, and they are much better value for money," he says.

"As an example, take Gary Glitter. A lot of the singles he puts out are fun, but they are very short-lived. But I'm sure some of the kids had no comprehension that Gary Glitter could actually sing a song like 'Happy Birthday' — until I played it from one of his albums on my radio programme. It's really an excellent piece of music."

His own taste in music? "I go for artists like Carly Simon, Elton John, Gordon Lightfoot, Neil Diamond. Fairly gentle music, which I recognise is not get-up-and-go music. But I like a song you can listen to four or five times without having heard everything on the record.

"I got some snide comments from one music paper because I said the Osmonds' latest album was one of the best produced albums of the year. I still think it had some very good music on it. But I realise too that in some quarters it's the wrong thing to say that you actually like the Osmonds in any way at all — which is all very stupid, and a lot of baloney. If I like an artist, then I say so."

Noel says he has changed a lot over the last year or so. "I went through a period of being a Very Angry Young Man. I was really quite stupid about it, because I was just being unprofessional. I wanted to make lots of changes in the radio programme I had.

"But I then realised that Radio-1 has a very definite policy, and I had to abide by it. I've now come to terms with this, and no matter what changes are made, I have to abide by the rules."

As well as being seen on Top of the Pops, of course, Noel has earned a big teenage and school-age fan following with his five-days-a-week breakfast programme on Radio-1.

"I think the biggest appeal the radio show has is to the twelve to sixteen age group, which is absolutely great because it's the same audience as Top of the Pops," says Noel.

And being bright and chirpy even at that time in the mornings may send youngsters off to school feeling that much more relaxed with Noel's brand of music-and-wit, but it also has its share of problems for our trendy young deejay.

"Often, I've not felt like being bright and cheerful and full of fun at that time in the morning," says Noel. "For a start, I have to get up at five o'clock every weekday, and drive to the BBC to be on the air by seven o'clock. I only see about half-a-dozen people before I'm on the air . . . and it's a very lonely time of the day. I'm usually coming out of the BBC, when everyone else is walking in to work.

"The biggest problem of all, though," he admits, "was in adapting to my own personal boredom. I realised that a lot of youngsters think it's great to be a disc jockey — and, of course, it is! But it can sometimes become very boring, too. Just like any other job.

"Just imagine the problem of basically playing similar records over and over again for several weeks. People listen to any programme, on average, for about twenty minutes or so. Whereas I'm putting on the same music, over and over again.

"I had to mentally adapt to playing the same sort of music over and over again, every day, especially when I'm doing ten hours of programmes throughout the week.

"You can have two months of playing and listening to the very same record, five times a week. And if it's not your particular kind of music, then it starts to get at you. I had to learn to fight this personal boredom."

What he'd like to do now, apart from Top of the Pops, says Noel, is tackle the News. But in a light-hearted way. "I'd like to try my hand at doing light-hearted news interviews. I think most people treat the news too seriously.

"Why shouldn't we laugh at the news more often? After all, it's not always quite as serious as news readers like to make out."

As a young man, he is very ambitious. He would like, he tells me, to one day open his own restaurant. He already has his own discotheque company, which provides the music at several different venues around London.

He has also taken up motor car racing as a hobby. He joined the Ford team, taking part in several saloon car races over the year. "I'm absolutely mad keen on cars," says Noel, who privately drives an Escort RS 2000.

From his new home in North London, he can actually now drive to the BBC's Broadcasting House in eight minutes. He once timed it. "But this meant going faster than I should, and although the roads are pretty deserted so early in the morning, I don't drive too fast any more," says Noel. "I would hate to be stopped for speeding, especially when I'm not in a great hurry."

When it comes to his appearances on Top of the Pops, Noel says, "I enjoy the show immensely. I'm a lot more relaxed now than I used to be. This all comes with experience.

"I sometimes feel I should try and be a bit sillier — have a few more laughs in front of the cameras. But it is very difficult when you are responsible for doing the links between the songs. There's not much time to fool about and stamp your own personality on the programme."

He recalls taking Tiddles, the lion cub, along with him to one programme last year. "Tom Jones was on the show that week, and I think this must have been the only time in Tom's career when the girls were turning away from him — to look at the little lion.

"There's only one fault with Top of the Pops," he says, with a chuckle. "It doesn't give me enough time, in between the numbers, to set up a proper comedy situation.

"Y'see, I'm really a frustrated TV comedian, and I'd like to do more comedy on television."

One young girl who was in the audience for Top of the Pops knows just what Noel means. Noel asked her, during the show, "Do you like surprises?" She innocently replied, "Yes."

He turned away from her, then suddenly turned round and shouted "Boooo!" Everyone in the studio roared with laughter — including the girl. That's what Noel means by being a zany character.

Dave Lee Travis

Dave Lee Travis admits it . . . "I'm a complete loony," he says. "An absolute nut case. I'll do anything for a laugh."

With his bubbling personality and roaring laugh, Dave brought a new brand of eccentricity and zany humour to Top of the Pops, when he was introduced as one of the programme presenters last year.

His voice, of course, was already familiar to radio listeners, and he had his own daily Radio-1 show. But he was new to television in this country . . . although by no means a newcomer to the medium.

Dave spent two-and-a-half years in Bremen, Germany, doing his own TV show, which pulled in an audience all over the Continent of some 80 million viewers.

He's been broadcasting for twelve years. He started off working in discos and nightclubs in and around Manchester, his hometown. Then he joined Radio Caroline pirate ship, working for two years on the southern ship, and six months on the northern ship, based off the Isle of Man.

It was while he was broadcasting on Radio Caroline that a German TV producer heard him, liked the sound of the voice, and quickly booked him for his own monthly TV show in Bremen.

"I used to specialise in being really nutty," says Dave. "I remember the first TV show I did. I walked up and unscrewed the camera lens. The cameraman was horrified, because the Germans have a very strange sense of humour. But then they suddenly all fell about, laughing . . . and I was 'away'.

"After that, they thought I was a nutter. A maniac. So I then used to do anything at all, just to get a laugh." He became known as Big Dave, the English Nut.

It was this infectious humour which he brought to Top of the Pops. On one of his very early shows, he suddenly leapt away from the microphone, joined the group Mud, and went berserk on the drums.

"I'm not just a DJ, I'm a really dedicated all-round entertainer," says Dave seriously. "It might sound a bit big-headed to say so, but I *know* I'm going to be a really big-name entertainer a few years from now. Just wait and see. I'll have a really monster TV show of my own."

He says it with such conviction, that you've just got to believe the lad.

"I'm the Roy Castle of the deejay world. I can do a bit of everything. Sing, dance, tell gags."

He runs his own disco shows, putting on a complete stage production, hiring dancers, and doing a full act, himself, which includes singing, playing music, and lots and lots of jokes.

"I do a lot of comedy in my stage shows. I may well finish up being a full-time comedian, in fact."

His road show is aimed at young people in the twenty to twenty-five age group. But his radio shows, he says, appeal to everyone — from the teenyboppers to Mums and Grandmas.

Dave is now affectionately known as "The Hairy Monster from 200 miles up the M1" — a title given to him, jokingly, by "Diddy" David Hamilton a few years back.

"They used to laugh at me because I came from Manchester, and drove down the M1 every week to do the radio shows in London," says Dave. Now, he lives in Ealing, North London, with his wife — a beautiful Swedish blonde called Marianne, and two cats — called Igor and Natasha.

Marianne came to Britain to work as an au-pair. She met Dave in a Manchester club on her very first night in England — "And it was the best thing that ever happened to me," says Dave, with that monster grin showing through his whiskers. "She keeps me reasonably sane."

He started his working life, straight from school, as a designer in a posh store in Manchester. But he gave it up, and went working in clubs as a teenage disc jockey for ten bob a night.

"I introduced the Beatles to their first Manchester audience," recalls Dave. "In a club called The Oasis."

Mad on motor cars, and drag racing in particular, DLT is a walking encyclopaedia on all kinds of music.

"I like virtually everything," he says. "But I prefer the more melodic type of artist. I love the Burt Bacharach kind of music, and I've been a great fan of Dusty Springfield for years.

"Kiki Dee is a great artist. I really dig her. Such an under-rated singer. I like Isaac Hayes — such a fantastic feeling for the music.

"But I don't care what kind of music people play or listen to — highbrow or lowbrow . . . so long as it's of a good standard. That's the important thing with all music."

Tony Blackburn

Tony Blackburn has picked up no fewer than two dozen awards over the last ten years or so.

Last year he was voted top Radio-1 disc jockey by readers of *Reveille* for the fifth year running. And this is something which Tony finds very gratifying.

"Everyone likes winning awards and coming top of the polls in popularity contests," he says. "It's only natural."

He's now been with Top of the Pops for seven years. And, like Jimmy Savile, Tony has branched out into other sides of show business. Last year, he did his first pantomime, playing Buttons in a stage production of "Cinderella" at East Ham, London — with the lovely Anne Aston from TV's "The Golden Shot" as Cinders.

His radio show, too, has changed, he says. Since he was married (to dishy young actress

With Top of the Pops now eleven years old, we asked DJ TONY BLACKBURN to look back over the last eleven years and give us his Top Eleven favourite records. Here is his choice. . . .

1 **"Reach Out, I'll Be There"**
                        — by The Four Tops.
2 **"Home Loving Man" — Andy Williams.**
3 **"Only Just Begun" — The Carpenters.**
4 **"Strawberry Fields Forever"**
                        — The Beatles.
5 **"I'm Still Waiting" — Diana Ross.**
6 **"Never Get to Heaven"**
                        — Dionne Warwick.
7 **"Save The Children" — Marvin Gaye.**
8 **"Baby Love" — The Supremes.**
9 **"Trains and Boats and Planes"**
                        — Burt Bacharach.
10 **"Raindrops Keep Falling On My Head"**
                        — Sacha Distel.
11 **"Rag Doll" — The Four Seasons.**

Tessa Wyatt) and became a family man (their son, Simon, is nearly two) Tony finds it much easier to talk to housewives — "because I now know some of the problems they have to face."

Says Tony: "As a bachelor, I used to quite enjoy doing my own housework, going shopping, and that sort of thing. But of course it was all only part-time. Once you're married, you realise that wives are often in the house all day — and they appreciate a friendly voice coming to them over the radio.

"I also understand children much more than I used to. Not only being a Dad, and having a baby toddling around the house, but also working in pantomime gave me great experience of working with youngsters. And this, of course, helps tremendously when it comes to doing Top of the Pops, and mixing with the youngsters in the studio audience."

Tony always does his own warm-up for the TV show. "I go on about half-an-hour before the show is due to start. I talk to the kids, get to know them, pick one or two out who I might want to talk to once the show is on the air.

"We play them some music, get them dancing, tell them how the cameras work and how the programme is produced. Because it is very confusing with cameras and microphones all over the place, particularly for youngsters who have never been in a TV studio before. I like to bring in one or two young people for a brief chat in between introducing the songs.

"But it can sometimes be pretty nerve-wracking, having so many youngsters all mobbing around you. It's not a particularly easy show to do . . . and my style is to relax as much as possible and have some fun with the kids."

In between his appearances on Top of the Pops, Tony also introduced a series of cartoon programmes on BBC, called "Cartoon Carnival". "I really enjoy doing programmes like that," he says. "In fact, I'd like to do more programmes for children."

Musically, Tony prefers a wide selection of artists right across the pop board, instead of just one particular section of pop. "On my Radio-1 programme I play the records of people like Jack Jones and Andy Williams, as well as the Top Thirty best sellers.

"I think artists like Gary Glitter are tremendous. And I like the Osmonds and David Cassidy.

"Progressive music has slid out, which I'm glad about. There was at one time too much progressive music in the charts, and, personally, I didn't like it. I think pop has now got back to good showmanship, and that's what I like. Artists are now working at building up a proper act, and dressing up. Not coming on simply dressed in dirty T-shirt and old jeans.

"That's the pop music scene . . . it's changing all the time."

Paul McCartney is one of the bravest artists around on the pop scene. He simply had to be tough – to take all the stick and criticism meted out to him when he split up from the Beatles, and then came back after six years in the wilderness to form his new group, Wings.

But he's proved, over the last year or two, that he still has that essential touch of talent which made him one of the finest song-writers the pop world has ever known.

Anyone who penned such songs as "Yesterday", "Michelle" and "Eleanor Rigby", now all pop classics, could never be forgotten, just like that!

That's why, when the whole musical world was busy attacking Paul McCartney for breaking up the Beatles, years after the big split, Paul was occupied in re-forming his musical ideas, re-thinking his future, and re-packaging a completely new band.

"When we split up, it was like getting out of the Army – for all of us," Paul said of the Beatles' break-up. "It hurt at first. I thought then it was the end of my career. We were all very angry. But now all is forgiven."

Of constant rumours and hopeful suggestions that the four lads from Liverpool – John, Paul, George and Ringo – would one day re-form, as the Beatles, Paul has always agreed that it was more than a mere possibility.

Clearly the four Scousers still have something in common – if it's only a love of the music they created. But the Beatles, as a rock 'n' roll quartet, frantically performing on stage, getting the little girls screaming with wild excitement, is a thing of the past.

With the formation of Wings, Paul seemed to arouse a great deal of antagonism, simply because he brought his wife, American-born Linda, into the group, when a lot of people obviously thought she was without experience and without any particular talent.

But all along, Paul has stood by her, repeatedly saying: "I like what Linda does. And she's learn-ing all the time as a musician."

Paul said, "I felt very naked for a while after the Beatles broke up. Some people said I failed to live up to my potential after I went out on my own, and probably they were right. But it's all coming back now. It really is.

"It was very difficult for some-body in my position to start a new band from scratch. But we either sat around and moped, or got on with it."

The old Paul McCartney has, quite clearly, sorted himself out. He's now happy, he says, simply producing the music he enjoys.

It may not be as vibrant, as immediately exciting as that "Mer-sey Sound" the four mop-haired Beatles produced a decade ago . . . but it's the McCartney Sound. And he's happy with it.

So are the punters. The people who flock to buy the records waxed by Wings.

Paul has always had hidden determination. Anyone who has worked closely with him will tell you this. He's never really been a "loner". He has always been much happier surrounded by a group.

This goes right back to his very first appearance on any stage – at a Butlin's holiday camp – when Paul was just eleven years old and went on stage with his guitar and sang "Long Tall Sally". Even then, he had to drag his kid brother Mike up on stage with him, to wail away – even though Mike had a broken arm in plaster at the time.

"Maybe I'm shy, but I work much better with somebody else on stage with me," says Paul.

But what his fans still like about McCartney is the way he came back with the new group. The actual way Wings made their bow, three years ago.

There was no blatant publicity. Paul deliberately avoided all the usual hassle of possible fan hys-teria. He simply got his group together – Denny Laine and Henry McCullough on guitars, Denny Seiwell on drums and Linda on tambourine – and they went out, quite unannounced, and started "doing their own thing".

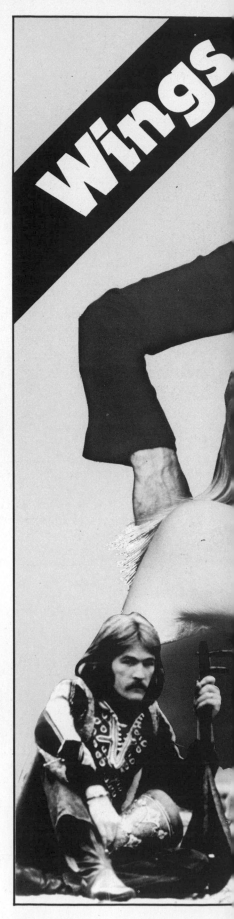

It's history now, of course. But they just arrived in Nottingham – because that looked a nice spot on the map, Paul and Linda said later – set up their equipment, and gave a spontaneous, free concert to students at Nottingham University.

From there on, they went out and about with a caravan and a truck, peddling their new musical sound. Getting experience together. Experimenting. Trying to get it right.

Since then, Paul and Linda and the group have really spread their Wings.

"Performing hasn't changed any since I went out with the Beatles," said Paul. "It's just a different band and different material. It could never change. Performing is performing. It's still just trying to put over a song . . ."

Linda has said of Paul: "After the Beatles finished, he was suddenly out of a job. It could have destroyed him if he hadn't been McCartney, the professional."

But Paul has always had this thing about not wanting to be a "yesterday's man". "I don't want to be like a retired general, talking about the last war," he said. "I don't want to be somebody who *was*. David Cassidy is *now*. People don't pass him in the street and say 'You know who he used to be!' I want to be part of today – not yesterday."

Since Wings were formed, of course, Linda McCartney, in particular, has gone from strength to strength. She's branched out as a singer in her own right. She, too, had to undergo a great deal of initial criticism.

"When I married Paul, I couldn't play anything," Linda has said. "My husband wanted me to play in the group. He forced me to play."

She practised, at home, playing various instruments, as well as the piano. And she gained confidence from Paul, she said, when it came to developing her own voice.

So that, despite the knockers – or maybe in an ironic way, because of them – the McCartneys are still very much around.

if it's black, it's really Beautiful...

KATY BARNES traces the history of black music – and looks at some of the finest black singers in the world of pop.

Just over a year ago, a new magazine was launched by the giant publishing company, IPC, called *Black Music*. That it even got past the planning stages is an important indication of the popularity of the black artist in Britain.

Of course, if you go back in history, all of today's pop music had its origins deeply rooted in the black culture which evolved out of America's Southern States at the time when the slave trade was at its height, and literally thousands of Africans, from all over that huge country, were crowded like cattle into old-time sailing ships and transported in the most primitive conditions to the New World.

About the only thing that they brought with them was their music. Ancient chants and rhythms which, over the years, became integrated with their new way of life and new language. Treated like illiterate children, all the slaves could do to relieve their misery and homesickness was to sing. And out of this came the blues.

After the American Civil War, the negroes began to have a little more freedom, and slowly left the big cotton plantations of the South and moved to the Northern industrial cities where work and money were more plentiful. They could begin to build themselves a better standard of living and a culture of their own within a black environment.

The major centres for the re-settlement of the black race were Detroit and Chicago, and with a change in the way they lived came a gradual change in music. Folk music, or the music of the people, which after all is the real definition, has always, since time began, reflected the life style of the musician. Therefore, the blues became urbanised and the introduction of instruments meant the blues were beginning to get more sophisticated.

Whilst this was going on in the North, New Orleans was growing into the traditional jazz centre of the world, through a similar kind of evolvement but in a slightly different direction. There, brass was beginning to play an important part in black music, and the streets and bars of the old French city transported to the new United States would echo to the strains of singers and musicians playing happy swinging music with a lot of vocal and instrumental improvisation.

So for a while jazz and blues developed along a parallel and very soon blues artists began to emerge on record, selling only at first to the ethnic population, but slowly over the years crossing over into the more popular fields. Labels like Chess, Chance, Jax, United and Flair began to appear on record shop counters, and the artists moved away from the street corners and into clubs and bars.

Then along came Sam Phillips and the Sun label, who cut people like the very young Elvis Presley, Roy Orbison, Carl Perkins and Jerry Lee Lewis – all white performers influenced by black blues singers. And so rock 'n' roll was born. Music to change the world.

Much later, white artists like Mick Jagger and the Rolling Stones were to be influenced by the major black artists of an earlier era – people like Chuck Berry, Bo Diddley and Muddy Waters. And this in turn marked a revival interest in the original singers who had been big names in the Fifties.

This white involvement was important to the development of black music because it then became exposed to a much wider audience. This meant it was now a more commercial proposition and so of interest to major record companies and distributors, who need to sell a lot of records to survive.

Nowadays black music is established in its own right all around the world, the basic categories being rhythm and blues (R & B), blues, soul, jazz and reggae. This last of course was developed by the negroes from Africa, who ended up on the sugar plantations of the West Indies, and has been introduced to Britain by the immigrants who began to move here after the last war. It is still relatively unknown, however, in America.

The first black artist to make a name as an international entertainer was a singer called Paul Robeson who, in the Thirties, appeared in such Hollywood movies as "Sanders of the River" and "Showboat" along with Alan Jones, father of American crooner Jack Jones. "Old Man River" became Robeson's song everywhere that records were sold, and he was successful in films and recording.

Louis Armstrong was obviously coming into things around the same time, as was Cab Calloway and his band (they played the London Palladium in 1936). Over the years, people like Duke Ellington, Rose Murphy, Fats Waller, Ray Ellington – particularly strong in the Fifties – the

Randy Jackson

Smokey
Robinson

Diana Ross

Peters Sisters, Hutch, the Ink Spots, the Deep River Boys, Billy Eckstein, Billy Daniels and Ella Fitzgerald, all became household names in Britain with sell-out concerts and chart records making them the superstars of their day.

By the time the late Fifties and Sixties arrived, the vogue was for vocal harmony groups like the Platters, the Orlons, the Flamingoes, the Moonglows and the Ronnettes — who incidentally were the very first black vocal group ever to appear on Top of the Pops, back in 1964, with their hit number "Baby I Love You".

But these were all groups who had individual sounds and recording contracts. Not until Tamla Motown happened was there a strong pop-oriented label, specifically for black artists, run by black people with writers, producers, arrangers and singers all under one roof. Tamla really revolutionised black music with talent like the Supremes, Smokey Robinson and the Miracles, Stevie Wonder, the Temptations and the truly amazing Jackson Five.

They opened the way for a massive invasion of the world charts by black singers and groups and paved the way for countless others on the road to fame and fortune, including the Stylistics, the Detroit Emeralds, and the newest act on the chart scene in this country, Limmie and Family Cookin'.

The Supremes had their first American No. 1 with "Where Did Our Love Go?", which was only their second single after leaving school and going on the road with the Motown Review.

Over a period of ten years, they had fifteen consecutive smashes in the record charts, and at one point made the No. 1 spot five times running. Their long string of gold discs includes "Baby Love", "Stop In The Name of Love", "Someday We'll Be Together". The Supremes became the No. 1 girl vocal group in the world. They were sensational, wherever they appeared, and were tagged "The top popstyle setters of the Sixties".

Diana Ross, Mary Wilson and Florence

The stylish Stylistics

Ballard, the original Supremes, got together in 1960 and auditioned for Berry Gordy, who was just starting the Tamla Motown company in Detroit. They began by backing Marvin Gaye and Mary Wells on record, but went on to become international stars in their own right.

In 1969, Diana left the group. As lead singer with the Supremes, she was part of the most phenomenally successful popular singing group in history. But she's since gone on to increase her reputation as a solo artist, with concerts around the world, television appearances and hit records.

About four years ago, Diana married rock manager Robert Silberstein, and with her two little daughters and her sister's son of whom she had custody, she admits to being a "home-bird" at heart. However, she has no plans to desert her many millions of fans, and is now getting more involved in music with the Jackson Five, whom she discovered, and with record production generally, starting with a couple of tracks on her album "Touch Me In The Morning", which was also the title of one of her million-selling singles.

Smokey Robinson and the Miracles were together for fifteen years before Smokey left them to play a more active part in the administration of the Tamla Corporation. It was in 1957 that the Miracles were first heard by Berry Gordy Jnr, who recognised their potential, and in fact it was with the Miracles that Motown had its first ever hit record. "Shop Around" was released in 1960 and became their first million-seller.

Smokey Robinson has been partly responsible for the whole Tamla Motown sound, working with most of the acts over the years. For instance, it was Smokey who produced "My Guy" with Mary Wells. He also writes and arranges to the extent that the distinctive Tamla Motown sound has proved to be the forerunner of the Philly Sound, even more updated with lots of lush strings and laid-back soulful vocals.

In 1964, the year in which the Miracles first visited Britain with the Motown Review, Smokey became vice-president of Tamla. The Review was used to introduce Motown to Europe, and in fact was filmed for a TV special with our own Dusty Springfield introducing it. Artists then included the Temptations, the Four Tops, the Supremes and Martha and the Vandellas.

Smokey Robinson is still recording as a solo singer, and not so long ago came up with his "Smokey" album containing mostly his own songs, apart from a couple written with Marv Tarplin, a guitarist who worked with the Miracles for some years.

"I'm still very concerned with the Miracles," says Smokey, "and I get involved in whatever they do." After all, he was responsible for many of their biggest hits, including "Mickies Monkey", "Tracks of My Tears" and "Tears of a Clown",

the last one making the British charts long before it was even released in America.

In just over ten years, Stevie Wonder has gone from the original child Motown superstar to one of the most diversified music makers in the contemporary field. Born blind, the third of six children, on 13th March 1950, Stevie began playing with musical instruments at the age of five. When he was twelve, one of the Miracles, Ron White, heard him playing harmonica and was so overwhelmed by his style that he took the young Stevie to meet Motown president Berry Gordy. Success was almost immediate for Little Stevie Wonder, as he was billed on the first record label. With his first No. 1, "Fingertips", at the age of thirteen, Stevie Wonder became the first teenager to sell a million records for Motown . . . and that was years before the Jackson Five!

Following "Fingertips", Stevie's list of hits is impressive: "Uptight", "I Was Made To Love Her", "For Once In My Life", "My Cherie Amour", "Yester-You, Yester-Me, Yesterday", "Never Had A Dream Come True", "Signed Sealed and Delivered".

His progress became increasingly obvious in his albums, but with "Signed, Sealed and Delivered", he made his mark as a producer for the first time, and followed that with "Where I'm Coming From", which saw the introduction of the synthesiser, soon to become the instrument he preferred to interpret his musical ideas.

Then came "Music Of My Mind", the album which really established him as a truly contemporary innovator and one which led to an invitation from the Rolling Stones to tour with them in the U.S.

Since then Stevie has come up with "Talking Book" and "Innervisions", both albums which show him to be an extraordinarily talented composer, arranger, producer and entertainer.

The Temptations, described as "the world's top male vocal group", went to Tamla Motown through singer Jackie Wilson. The Temps have been together more than twelve years, and got their first taste of things to come as a vocal "fill in" group on rock 'n' roll package shows in a local Detroit theatre for a mere fifteen dollars each.

They have since become an institution, with a long list of hit records to their credit: "The Way You Do The Things You Do", "I'll Be In Trouble", "My Girl", and their biggest for some years "Papa Was A Rollin' Stone", to name just a few.

"We like to sing about life," say the Temptations. "Love songs, although beautiful, are usually unreal." The Temptations are made up of Dennis Edwards, Richard Street, Damon Harris, Otis Williams and David English.

Twice they've lost important members of the group — David Ruffin in 1968 and Eddie Kendricks in 1970 — but through hard work and determination, each time they re-built the act and

stayed on top.

Lastly, talking about Tamla people, are the fantastic Jacksons, not only the first black teeny-bop act but one of the world's foremost attractions these days — along with, of course, the Osmonds and David Cassidy — on the whole Teen Scene.

First brought to Motown by Diana Ross, she was introduced to them by the Mayor of Gary, Indiana, the boys' hometown. The Jacksons' father, Joe, had been playing in a local group out of Chicago back in the Fifties, mostly blues.

The young Jacksons would listen to rehearsals, and there were always various musical instruments around. Eventually, Joe turned the house over to the children's music, and admits that he used to be in trouble with Mrs. Jackson for spending too much money on instruments for all the boys.

First, it was the three elder sons, Jackie, Tito and Jermaine. But after Marlon and Michael joined the group, they won a talent contest at Roosevelt High School, and over the next few years entered and won several competitions.

They used to play five nights a week in local theatres around Gary and in Chicago, with groups like the Emotions and the Chi Lites. By the time Diana Ross first introduced the boys on stage at Beverley Hills in 1969, the group was reported to have a "repertoire that ranges from Ray Charles to Charles Aznavour".

Ever since their first hit single "I Want You Back", the Jackson Five have become a kind of super teeny group with one successful record after another: "A.B.C.", "The Love You Save", "I'll Be There", "Mama's Pearl", "Never Can Say Goodbye", followed by just as many albums.

Michael and Jermaine have also had their own singles and albums out, both here and in America.

Success was not too long in coming for the Jackson boys, but they did have problems with fitting in school work. So they toured with their own tutor when not reporting in at school. Somehow, they have managed to fit in their studies while continuing with their fantastic musical career.

Michael now wants to take art in college, and Jackie wants to go to business school. But they're still making happy music, and with little Randy now starting on percussion and vocals, they look certain to hold their position among the top teen groups for some years yet.

The Detroit Emeralds — from the motor city — have been together for many years — ever since their schooldays, in fact, back in 1966. Brothers Abrim and Ivory Tillmon met up with James Mitchell Jnr, after moving from Little Rock, Arkansas, to Detroit. Prior to becoming the Detroit Emeralds, they were known as the Tillmon Brothers, one of the top gospel groups in town.

The Emeralds all sing lead. Depending on the

song, they change around with the other two doing the harmony line, and for recording they are sometimes joined by another Tillmon brother — Cleofas — who has an exceptionally high tenor voice.

The recording career of the Emeralds is somewhat chequered. But in 1969 the group signed with a new label, Westbound. Their first single did nothing, but the next one — "If I Love Your Love" — produced by the boys themselves, began to break through, though it wasn't until 1971 and "Do Me Right" that they had their first American chart smash.

Then came "Wear This Ring", and "You Want It You Got It", their first million-seller. At this time the Detroit Emeralds were pretty much unnoticed over here, despite a British tour early in 1972.

"You Want It You Got It" was followed last year by two more British chart entries, "Feel The Need" and "I Think of You", continuing their position as one of the best soul groups to become a British name.

For the Stylistics it all began at High School in Philadelphia. James Smith, Herb Murrell, Russell Thompkins, Airion Love and James Dunn got together as the Stylistics, singing in local clubs.

But national recognition did not come until "You're A Big Girl Now", which they recorded in 1970.

This record topped the black charts in America and soon white radio stations began playing the Stylistics, causing quite a stir with record buyers all over the States.

The group then got together with Thom Bell, a producer who had made that other Philly Soul act, the Delfonics. And from the very first session, the Stylistics never looked back.

From their very first album came no less than four single chart entries, "Stop, Look And Listen", "Betcha By Golly Wow", "People Make The World" and "You Are Everything", some of which also made the British charts.

Apart from the Delfonics, the Stylistics were really the first vocal group to get that up-town slow soulful Philly sound high into the charts — certainly in this country, anyway.

The "Round 2" album followed the first and another British hit, "Rockin' Roll Baby", meant that the five boys from Philadelphia had added another page to the history of black music, whilst making new friends on both sides of the Atlantic.

They were widely acclaimed in England on their promotional tour of 1973, when they filmed their first appearance for Top of the Pops.

You may wonder why all the activity and exciting new sounds in the world of black music seem to come from America. Well, actually that's not completely true, as our own Hot Chocolate regularly release chart-making records. Johnny Nash and Desmond Dekker, both of whom base themselves here, have come out with hit records, whilst there are record labels like Beacon and Trojan that release reggae music. So far though there is only one company, Fresh Air Records, devoted specifically to breaking Black British Soul, and it could well be a label to watch out for.

Limmie and Family Cookin' are the latest black act to break through in this country with a "sleeper" record, "You Can Do Magic", which took seven months to enter the charts. Limmie and the two girls were born in Alabama but soon moved to Canton, Ohio. Limmie was the first to break out professionally and was recording for various labels from the age of eleven. Meanwhile the girls had been getting it together as the Sugarcakes.

The two sisters then teamed up with their brother and they were heard by a guy in a club in Cleveland. He is now their manager, and he obtained a contract for them with Avco Records, the same label that had been successful with the Stylistics. The first single from Limmie and Family Cookin' didn't happen for them in the States, but it became a hit over here, making No. 3 spot at the time the group undertook their first British tour, as well as an appearance on Top of the Pops.

That record earned them a silver disc — "the first time we were ever awarded anything in our whole lives," quipped Limmie. Although Limmie and Family Cookin' are not yet into the really Big Time, their distinctive pop soul sound should still be around in years to come.

However, if black music is your interest, stick with it. There are lots of beautiful records available. And lots of good artists and groups coming up. Let's hope we'll be seeing many more of them in the charts — and therefore on Top of the Pops throughout the next year.

Stevie Wonder

QUIZ

So you think you know it all
when it comes to the pop scene?
Try this quiz — and find out
just how smart you are.

1 Who was leader of the Spiders From Mars?
2 Who said "The Show Must Go On"?
3 Which now famous singer once recorded under the name of Neil MacArthur?
4 Who wrote the hit songs "Calendar Girl", "Oh Carol" and "Breaking Up Is Hard To Do"?
5 David Cook is now better known as — who?
6 Who wrote Mott The Hoople's first big single "All The Young Dudes"?
7 What are the names of the youngest members of the Osmonds and the Jacksons?
8 Carly . . . Kiki . . . Lynsey? Surnames, please.
9 Who sang "Hello, Hello, I'm Back Again"?
10 Dan McCafferty, Pete Agnew, Manual Charlton and Darrell Sweet . . . which group?
11 When Peter Doyle left the New Seekers, who took his place?
12 Who is the female singer in Blue Mink?
13 Can you name the first group Colin Blunstone played with?
14 Who is lead singer with Mott The Hoople?
15 Who made his debut with a song called "I Love My Dog"?
16 Phil Lynott, Eric Bell, Brian Downey — which group?

17 Which group first found chart success with "Crazy"?
18 The song "Alexander Graham Bell" was a big hit for which group?
19 What is Barry Blue's real name?
20 Which top group did Junior Campbell used to sing with?
21 Which group went to the top of the charts with "Part Of The Union"?
22 Who wrote and recorded "Papa Do"?
23 Scotsman Brian Connolly is lead singer with which group?
24 What group do Pete, Keith, Roger and John form?
25 Which group made the charts with "All The Way To Memphis" and "Honaloochie Boogie"?
26(a) Who produced a film of Marc Bolan?
   (b) What was it called?
27(a) What is David Bowie's real name?
   (b) What instrument does he play besides guitar?
28(a) Who is David Cassidy's stepmother?
   (b) What is Cassidy's Christian name in "The Partridge Family" TV series?
29 Can you name Andy Williams' nephews, who are now a singing duo?
30 Can you name the Mud line-up?

(ANSWERS ON PAGE 77)

CARPENTERS

Masters of their craft!

It's the Carpenters versus . . . say, Alice Cooper!

For all those parents who can't stand the sight of Alice Cooper and long-haired way-out groups like them, there is one singing group who present an exactly opposite image to the weird clothes and outrageous stage gimmicks . . . the Carpenters.

They're "the goodies". They portray everything that's good and clean and healthy about American youth.

Yet, strangely enough, they are as popular with the young kids as they are with older record buyers.

The Carpenters – brother and sister Richard and Karen Carpenter – have now been riding high in the States for the last five years or so. And over the last year or two, they've become without a doubt the most popular singing duo on both sides of the Atlantic.

Image-wise, they represent everything that's clean and wholesome. Even their publicity is highly geared to promoting this friendly Boy-and-Girl-Next-Door image. Which is fine, provided the couple have talent as well. A quality the Carpenters undoubtedly do possess.

At the age of twenty-eight and twenty-four, Richard and Karen Carpenter can already lay claim to a batch of gold records. You couldn't count their number of gold discs unless you use the fingers on more than two hands.

Their fans, they claim, range from teenyboppers to bridge-playing grandmothers. And I can well believe that.

They have that golden touch about everything they do. They only have to wax a new record – be it single or LP – and, almost certainly, it turns into gold for them and becomes an instant best-seller in the charts.

When it comes to their image thing, both Richard and Karen are quite adamant. A spokesman for them says categorically: "They know just what's happening. But unlike many of their musical peers, they don't feel the need to be negative about it, to rebel, or to tout convention by outlandish dress, stage manners and hairstyles.

"They don't 'put people on', and they don't put folk down. For the Carpenters, being 'high' means a natural, spirited buoyancy that needs no aid from chemical preparations. And this comes through, even in their music."

Strong words. But fair enough. That is simply the way the American couple like to play things.

There's no doubt, though, that the Carpenters did manage, against tremendous odds, to break through the Sound Barrier, foisting their soft, upbeat, melodic sound on to a pop public which was much more accustomed to the sound of heavy hard-rock.

Richard and Karen hail from New Haven, Connecticut, where they grew up. Their father was an avid collector of Dixieland jazz and big band records. The "sound" must have rubbed off on to little Richard, for at twelve the kid began playing the piano, and four years later he was studying classical piano at Yale, whilst saying he was twenty and doing gigs in local jazz clubs.

As for Karen, she was barely sweet sixteen when she, too, caught the music bug – and took up playing the drums. It wasn't long before she became one of the best – and certainly the loveliest – female drummers in Southern California.

In 1965, the Carpenter Trio was launched, with Richard on piano, Karen on drums, and a friend, Wes Jacobs, on tuba and bass.

The unknown trio entered the Hollywood Bowl Battle of the Bands, Los Angeles' non-pro musical contest . . . and calmly walked off with several trophies.

But they weren't quite satisfied with the sound they were producing, and Richard and Karen added some more guys to the group and completely repackaged their sound in the form of a sextet called Spectrum.

Although they then had a fine sound going for them they were up against a tremendous output of hard-rock from other groups. And so the Spectrum group split up.

Then came the Carpenters' move into the recording business. Karen started singing, Richard started writing some original songs, and greatly influenced, they admit, by the Beatles, the Beach Boys, the Bee Gees and Burt Bacharach, they came up with yet another new sound. They started experimenting with multi-track recording.

Richard and Karen blended their singing voices into four, six and eight parts. They then went the rounds of record producers with their tape. But they were turned down by everyone – except Herb Alpert, who heard the tape, thought it was a great sound . . . and Richard and Karen were promptly signed on contract by A & M Records.

Since then, they've never looked back. From their very first album for the record com-

pany, titled "Ticket To Ride", they found a sympathetic affinity with the American listening public. Then came another album, "Close To You". The title song, a Burt Bacharach composition, became a smash single. And "We've Only Just Begun" exploded soon after. These were the start of a string of ten golden records on the trot for the singing Carpenters.

Their warm, melodious sound quickly endeared them to a complete cross-section of the public.

They really knew they'd arrived when their third album, "Carpenters", hit the million selling mark within only three weeks of being released. And their fourth LP, "A Song For You", earned a gold disc the very day it was released into the shops. They followed this with another gold album, "Now And Then".

When they visited Australia, the Orient, and also came to Europe – and appeared on Top of the Pops in London – they were showered with further adulation. It was then the Carpenters knew they'd made it as truly international stars.

They are home-loving youngsters, and there is none of the big-star bit about either Richard or Karen. They live with their parents in a beautiful home in Downey, California, where they

have had a recreation wing added on to the house, plus two apartment complexes (appropriately named "Only Just Begun" and "Close To You", after two of their biggest song hits).

The Carpenters don't like the idea of ever "playing Superstars", they insist. Their fan mail has now reached teenybopper proportions, and Richard has become the heart-throb of millions of girls, women in their late teens and early twenties, as well as schoolgirls.

Karen's name has been linked romantically with that of Alan, of the Osmond brothers.

In spite of obvious fan worship, Richard insists that he has very definite tastes when it comes to girl friends. "The ideal girl for me has got to be a knockout to look at; with natural beauty. I hate lots of make-up," he says. "She's got to be slim. I usually go for girls with long hair, and I'm kinda partial to blondes."

He also likes, he says, girls who are talkative and with a strong sense of humour. "I get bored with girls who can't initiate a conversation, or who just give you one-word answers."

And the future Mrs. Carpenter, Richard always points out, must share his passion for cars. He currently has four of them in the garage, all different models.

Suddenly, its middle of the road Music...

Once upon a time music was divided up into "highbrow" and "lowbrow". The higher the brow presumably meant you had a bigger brain capacity needed to concentrate on classical music, while pea-brained lowbrows were satisfied with the less demanding popular jazz and dance music of the day.

Then along came "modern" jazz which needed even more brain power than a Mahler symphony demanded; and popular music became "pop".

And with the advent of rock 'n' roll even pop music began to get serious and new categories were created: Psychedelic, Underground, Contemporary, all eventually gave way to the all-embracing rock music of today.

But then pop music for the fun of it bounced back, and with it the need for yet another new category Teenybop music.

So now we have classical, jazz, pop and teeny-bop. But there is another massive area of music which takes a little bit from each of these categories and pleases a vast army of record-buyers and music-lovers.

In the old days it would have been called middle-brow. Today it has been dubbed middle-of-the-road music because it drives a course through the various extremes of music, producing a sound that is easy on the ear but nonetheless satisfying artistically.

Middle-of-the-road — or MOR as it is known in the trade — is sometimes despised by the serious music lover, be he a classical or rock aficionado, and indeed MOR music at its worst is nothing more than aural wallpaper.

The bland orchestral versions of pop hits and pop standards churned out relentlessly by

Neil Sedaka

endless tape cartridges in restaurants, super-markets, hotels and even lifts, gives MOR music a bad name and should be ignored (unless you are living ten years ahead of your time and 1985 is with us already!).

But that doesn't mean to say that orchestral music of this kind isn't worth listening to, as long as it is done well. The orchestras of Messrs. Mancini, Mantovani, Lefevre, Last, Alpert and Kaempfert, are all prime examples of excellent arrangements and superb instrumentation, very often bringing a new dimension of sophistication to an otherwise routine pop song.

Many millions of albums by the above-named gentlemen, and others like them, are bought by people who appreciate entertaining music. The marketing men in the music business have a theory that a lot of this sort of music is bought by Mums and Dads who have forked out for a record-player for their youngsters and get hooked on records themselves, or rediscover the pleasure of listening after a decade of TV watching.

Much middle-of-the-road music is also bought, appropriately enough, by car drivers in tape form. The soothing strings or lively rhythm section can calm the nerves in a traffic jam or keep you awake on a motorway.

And every so often a particularly catchy piece of orchestral or instrumental music can suddenly grab the nation's attention and start selling as a hit single, making a mockery of the pop charts.

Then it is Top of the Pops — and big TV exposure!

It is usually a TV or cinema theme which, heard repeatedly week after week, sticks in the mind and is whistled or hummed by everybody from messenger-boys to bank managers. Remember the Simon Park Orchestra's "Eye Level" which dominated the singles' chart for several weeks back in 1973?

And what about that amazing record-breaking "Amazing Grace", which turned the pipes and drums of the Royal Scots Dragoon Guards into worldwide pop stars for months on end in 1972?

In this country, too, a lot of Country and Western music would never be accepted unless it was dressed up as middle-of-the-road music. Tom Jones, Val Doonican, Ken Dodd and, of course, Elvis Presley have all had big hits with country-type songs. And a few actual country singers — notably the late Jim Reeves, Glen Campbell and Lynn Anderson — have managed to break into the vast MOR market with hit records.

A lot of good music laps over into MOR — and, vice versa, good MOR music can be readily accepted by pop enthusiasts.

In this category, the names of Nilsson, Neil Sedaka, Elton John and Gilbert O'Sullivan spring to mind.

Gilbert O'Sullivan

Elton John

Nilsson has a dedicated following of rock fans through his "Schmilsson" and "Son of Schmilsson" albums, but his single "Without You" was a No. 1 hit because it appealed to a much wider audience. And then Nilsson went on to step firmly into the middle-of-the-road itself with his "Little Touch of Schmilsson In The Night" album of old-time songs backed by a lush orchestra.

Gilbert O'Sullivan was hailed as a brilliant new songwriter by the serious pop papers a few years ago, but his hit singles are just as popular on the Jimmy Young Prog. as on "Sounds of the Seventies".

But perhaps Neil Sedaka represents the most obvious example of how pop and MOR music can be one and the same thing. Heart-throb of the Fifties and early Sixties with his hits like "Happy Birthday Sweet Sixteen" and "Calendar Girl", Sedaka bounced back a year or so ago with his "Emergence" and "Solitaire" albums.

Now a tubby, cherub-faced man in his thirties, Sedaka could wow an audience at London's Talk of the Town — bastion of middle-class middle-of-the-roadness — and at the same time win fulsome praise from the pop papers for his contemporary writing with songs like "Superbird", "I'm A Song (Sing Me)" and "That's When The Music Takes Me". A fabulous performer.

You could hardly imagine anyone more MOR than 60-odd-year-old daddy of the crooners, Perry Como, and yet it was with the songs of young contemporary writers Kris Kristoferson and Don McLean that he held court in the singles' chart over the last year or so.

And Jack Jones, regarded by many as a natural successor to Frank Sinatra, and a leggy, handsome feller to boot, recorded a whole album of songs written by the contemporary group Bread, and now commands the respect of the entire music business for his sheer technical ability as a singer.

Even the Beatles are MOR these days. At least those early melodic songs of Lennon and McCartney, like "Michelle" and "Fool On The Hill", which translate superbly to the treatment of the orchestras and voices of Henry Mancini, James Last, Matt Monro, Sergio Mendes and even the Boston Pops Symphony Orchestra.

Today's teenybop music too could easily be classified as middle-of-the-road, what with the various Osmonds and David Cassidy reviving songs that were crooned by Mums and Dads a few decades back when the Moon was much in demand as a partner for June in song lyrics.

All of which proves that good music should simply be called music. We should do away with all the pigeon-holes and categories and accept a song or a singer purely on their merits.

Because be it MOR, rock or classic, it's music to the ears of someone, somewhere. . . .

WHAT THE STARS SAY...

Some of the clever / witty / surprising / sad / awful / / cheerful things the pop people say from time to time.

MICK JAGGER

"I don't have very much money. I just spend it all."

ROY WOOD

"What matters is what goes on 'inside' your head. Not what it looks like from the outside."

TOM JONES

"I once saw David Bowie in a discotheque in London, and I couldn't believe it. He looked so pale and fragile. I guess women must want to mother him or something."

PAUL McCARTNEY

"Really, the only barometer you have is sales. If people buy your records, then they must like the music you're producing, which is all that matters. The thing I'm in isn't like art, where Van Gogh could struggle all his life and only be recognised after he died. I'm in a very immediate type of work."

DAVID ESSEX

"If it hadn't been for music, I might have ended up in jail . . ."

GARY GLITTER

"When I want to relax, I like nothing better than to pull on a pair of waders, a sweater and an old hat, and sit by a river bank for hours on end . . . just fishing."

LEO SAYER

"I'm a schizophrenic, really, like a clown — happy on the outside and sad on the inside. I'm quite happy really, but whenever I turn my mind to music, or once I go on stage, I go into a whole emotional trip. I'm a blues singer really, and my whole life comes out in just that hour on stage."

OLIVIA NEWTON-JOHN

"I don't really like heavy music."

KEITH RICHARD

"It's energy, it's electricity, it's whisky and a few other things . . . they're just words. If there's a good band on a good night, they swing, things happen. Mystique is not going to be mystique if you define it. If it's definable, it's not mystique."

CHARLIE WATTS

"I enjoy the actual playing, but I can't stand the hotel rooms and the living out of suitcases that goes with touring. If I was the leader of the Stones, we'd still be playing at little clubs in London."

ROD STEWART

"I enjoy spending money. I don't waste it. I wouldn't say I'm mean — but there are times when I've got long pockets and short arms."

DAVID BOWIE

"Everything I do is ploughed back into anything that can give me a constructive area in which to work as a creative artist. We will take gambles that very few other people will take. We've always been sink or swim. I hate being safe. I've never been safe. We take enormous gambles. I'm always on the point of not knowing whether I'm going to have anything when I wake up tomorrow morning."

SUZI QUATRO

"I'm still very much a girl. I keep hoping I'm going to meet a Greek god, but all I keep meeting are these guys in make-up."

NEIL SEDAKA

"When I was around in the Fifties they were tempestuous days. But I wouldn't like to go back to them. I was too young and naive and impressed with it all to be able to cope. Now I know how to handle it and am more tolerant. When people ask me about 'the good old days', I tend to throw them by saying 'You mean NOW?' The future — not the the past — is my scene."

letters

The Production staff answer some of your most consistent questions. . . .

Like all popular programmes, Top of the Pops attracts a huge postbag each week, the joy and despair of the production team. Joy because everyone connected with the programme is thrilled to know that so many viewers are sufficiently interested in it to write to the BBC (even if some of the letters aren't very complimentary!). And despair because so many people forget to put their addresses, or even names, on their letters, which means we can't reply to them – while the writers probably sit at home wondering why their letters are never acknowledged.

What do people write about? Criticism, suggestions, questions, every aspect of the programme gets covered one way or another and some of your letters are very funny indeed.

Lots of people write asking to see more of their favourites, or wanting an unknown group to be given a chance. But that's not what the programme is about, as Robin Nash, the producer, explains. Animals on the show always provoke a lot of letters, and some hardy perennials crop up over and over again:

QUESTION: "WHY AREN'T PAN'S PEOPLE ON EVERY WEEK?"

ANSWER: Although it may seem to you at home that the girls are simply flitting about the studio as the spirit takes them, their dances are actually carefully rehearsed, which means they must choose a record to dance to a week in advance. So with the programme's strict rule of playing only records going up the charts, if the one Pan's People have chosen has moved down during the week they've been rehearsing, it's out – just like that! Another reason, of course, is that even the BBC slave drivers feel that the girls are entitled to a few weeks' holiday each year!

Q: "HOW DO I BECOME A PAN'S PERSON?"

A: About as easily as becoming the first woman Prime Minister. Auditions are extremely rare and confined to fully trained dancers. You stand a slightly better chance of becoming one of the Young Generation, since they recruit new dancers quite often – but only from people who have been through a gruelling dancing school discipline and training.

Q: "WHY HAVE YOU NEVER HAD ELVIS PRESLEY ACTUALLY APPEARING ON THE PROGRAMME?"

A: Certainly not from lack of trying. Elvis' performances have always been severely restricted, in order to increase the effect when he does appear. Sadly, we've never been able to persuade him of the importance of Top of the Pops – although we've tried every kind of blandishment. This applies to other American artists too. Some of them have demanded more money than the cost of a month of programmes.

Q: "WHY IS TOP OF THE POPS NOT AS GOOD AS IT USED TO BE?"

A: This usually comes from eighteen-year-olds who have been watching the programme since they were little kids – they've outgrown it. Temporarily. A few more years and they'll be back amongst the huge audience of Mums and Dads who pretend to disapprove of the show, yet wouldn't miss it for anything.

Q: "ARE THE GROUPS MIMING TO THEIR RECORDS?"

A: No. The Musicians' Union forbids it – and they send observers to the studio to make sure nobody breaks the rule. However, since the production of records gets more and more complicated, groups are allowed to make a backing track first in order to produce the same kind of sound, so long as they sing "live" on the show.

Q: "HOW CAN I GET TICKETS TO BE ON THE SHOW?"

A: By writing to Top of the Pops at the Television Centre, Wood Lane, London, W.12, and being incredibly patient and persevering. Tickets are free, but are limited by G.L.C. safety regulations to 120 a week and the waiting list runs into months. The audience must be over sixteen and under twenty-six and they must be prepared to join in and dance. We recently had a letter asking us to put an eighteen-month-old baby on the waiting list. But generally, if you keep trying, it shouldn't take quite that long!

Q: "PLEASE CAN YOU SEND ME A PHOTOGRAPH / AUTOGRAPH / SOUVENIR OF MY FAVOURITE SINGER?"

A: Sorry, we can't help, much as we'd love to. People pay the BBC licence money to make programmes, not to hand out pop souvenirs. Your best bet is to write to the record company, since most of them are equipped to deal with fan mail.

So now you know some of the answers. But don't stop writing to us. We really enjoy your letters.

ROLLING

Charlie Watts

Mick Jagger once said that he would either retire or re-think his career when he was thirty-three.

Well, he hasn't long to go. He's now thirty-one.

And although many people may well think that the controversial rock 'n' roller has mellowed over the years, he's certainly not set yet for retirement, or an old rocking chair.

The Rolling Stones are still very much bowling along. And they still seem to know where it's at.

On their last American stage tour, they were hailed unashamedly as "the world's greatest rock 'n' roll band". And neither Jagger or any of his fellow Stones would argue with that.

The Stones have become an enigma. Outdated, it was thought not so very long ago. But they can still turn it on just whenever the mood takes them. Younger bands may well make the singles chart more often. But the Stones are still active enough not to be gathering moss.

On the recording scene, they do much better selling albums than on singles. And when it comes to doing a stage show, they can still pack 'em in at Wembley Stadium – 40,000 fans at a time!

In America, the kids queued up for twenty-four hours for tickets for their stage show, and then paid up to forty-five dollars apiece for seats.

Yet despite this undoubted popularity – or maybe because of it – the Stones have still not be-come fully accepted. Way, way back from their early start – when their manager Andrew Oldham built them up with the subtle thought-provoking slogan "Would you let your daughter marry a Rolling Stone?" – they've had to fight all along the way for whatever success that they've achieved.

Pilloried in the Press, the Stones have always, it seemed, had a penchant for attracting very bad publicity.

"But I've no regrets at all," says Mick Jagger. "I have never made a conscious effort to establish an image, so I am hardly in a position to have regrets about the one I've got. People like to typecast you, and they always will."

He still feels, he says, the same way he has always felt, since he started out in the business at the age of eighteen. "I wouldn't say I'm mellowed at all. But now I just want to get on with being a musician. Unfortunately, you just can't decide to stop being controversial."

A year ago, the Stones went back on the road into Europe – in a big way. It was their first concert tour in Europe for more than three years. They did a twenty-city, two month tour which was seen by nearly half-a-million rock-worshipping fans of all ages.

Since their first success – a dozen years ago – the Stones, it is estimated, have earned close on £100 million, and they've sold more than 40 million records.

STONES

Mick Jagger

Bill Wyman

Keith Richard

They've become the anti-heroes of pop music. The hero of every youngster who liked to call himself a rebel. The Stones, it has been said, cultivated, perhaps deliberately, a narcissistic nastiness and a paranoic dislike of the society that bred them.

Younger artists – like Rod Stewart and David Bowie – may well think they have taken over the mantle. But the Stones still prove, by their very Box Office attraction, that they still have a unique magnetism. They still play to capacity houses on any concert tour.

And Jagger, it is said, is still probably the most sensuous and sexual solo performer in his particular pop field.

They may well have started out being hated by society and the Establishment, but Jagger, one feels, is now accepted socially. He frequently mixes in high-society circles. But there is still, one suspects, a hesitation on the part of many Mums and Dads about the merits of Mr. Jagger. They still don't know whether Mick Jagger is safe or not as a hero for their offspring.

It was the late Brian Jones, the brilliant guitarist, who first formed the Rolling Stones. At that time, he wasn't even sure whether Mick Jagger would be right for them.

Ian Stewart, the Rolling Stone who missed out on fame and fortune, was one of the original members of the group, before they turned fully professional. He recalls: "I remember the first time I saw Mick Jagger. His voice wasn't so great, but even then he had this charisma. There was nobody else like him."

But Brian wasn't so sure about him. He actually wanted Paul Jones (ex-Manfred Mann group) for the Stones, but couldn't get hold of him.

It's difficult now, of course, to even imagine the Rolling Stones without Mick Jagger!

How has the record industry changed since the Stones started? Says Mick: "When we started, rock 'n' roll was rather drab. That's why I never thought of being a rock 'n' roll singer, because it was a very draggy thing to be at that time.

"This was before the Beatles. That in-between period after Eddie Cochran and before the Beatles was a very dumb period. The business was just like a number of little boys running around being groomed for stardom – that's basically what it was.

"We just decided to play blues at that time, and that was a very uncommercial thing.

"Then the whole thing of LP records happened. People started to listen to more than two minutes of our music."

And it was Top of the Pops which really shot the Rolling Stones to stardom.

Which is something for which Mick and the other Stones will be eternally grateful.

Ronnie Laine

Status Quo – John Coglan

HEART-

Olivia Newton-John

Noel Edmonds

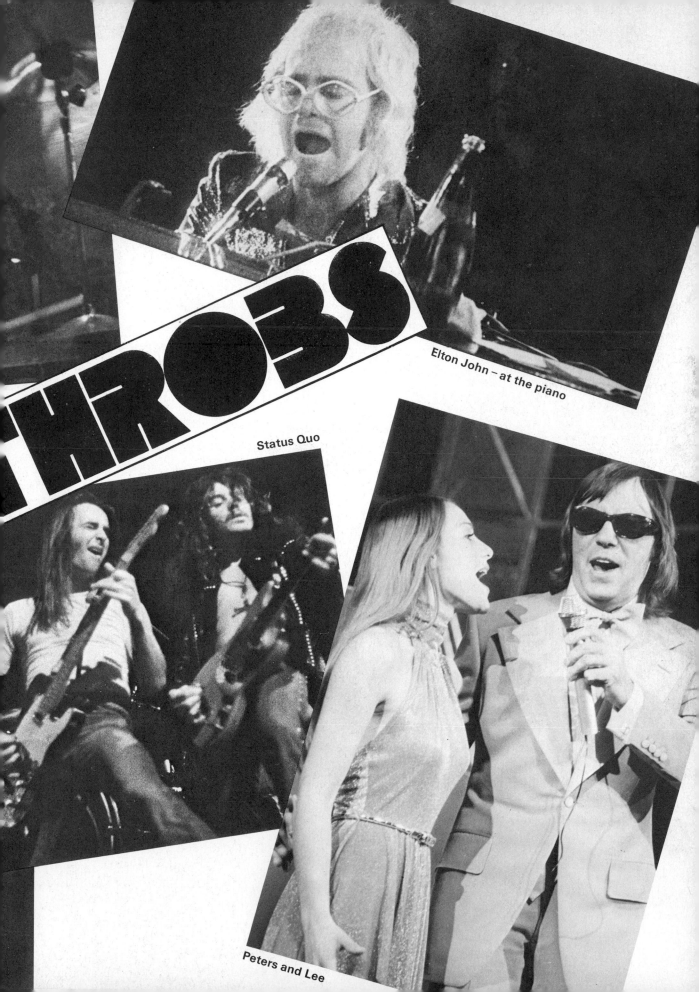

THROBS

Elton John – at the piano

Status Quo

Peters and Lee

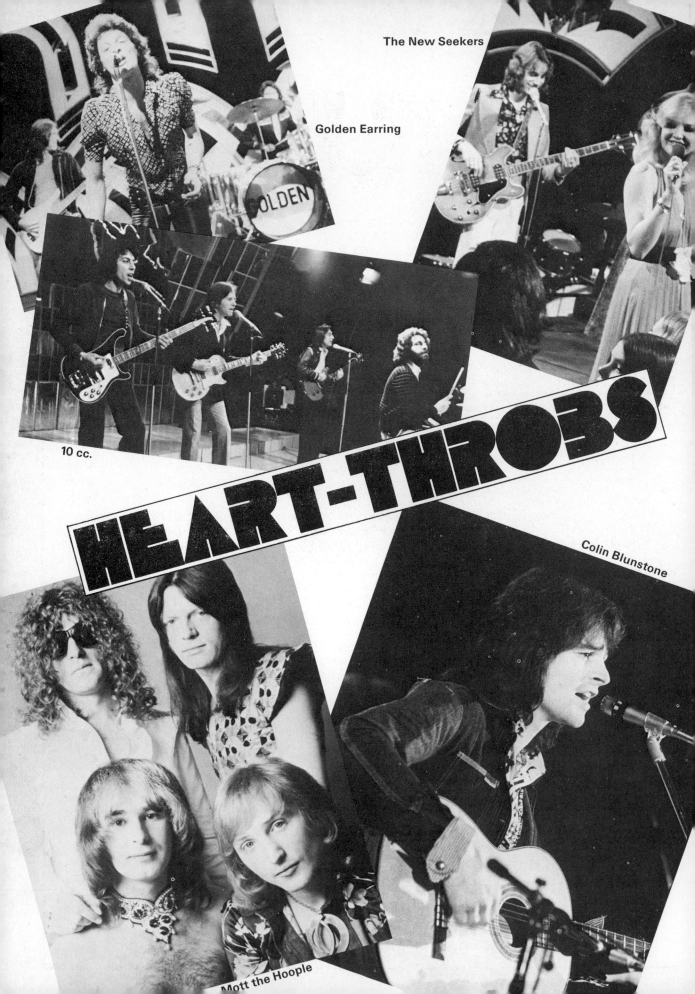

The New Seekers

Golden Earring

10 cc.

HEART-THROBS

Colin Blunstone

Mott the Hoople

Answers

TO I RECOGNISE THAT FACE

1 Gerry and the Pacemakers. Their hit records included: "I Like It", "You'll Never Walk Alone", "Ferry Cross The Mersey", "Don't Let The Sun Catch You Crying", "How Do You Do It?", "I'm The One".

2 Brian Poole and the Tremeloes. "Do You Love Me?", "Someone", "Candy Man", "Twelve Steps To Love", "Twist And Shout", "I Can Dance", "Here Comes My Baby", "(Call Me) Number One", "Hello World".

3 The Swinging Blue Jeans. "The Hippy Hippy Shake", "Too Late Now".

4 The Searchers. "Needles and Pins", "Don't Throw Your Love Away", "Sweets For My Sweet", "Sugar And Spice", "Ain't Gonna Kiss You", "Someday We're Gonna Love Again", "When You Walk In The Room", "What Have They Done To The Rain?", "Goodbye, My Love".

5 Dusty Springfield. "I Only Want To Be With You", "Wishin' And Hopin'", "You Don't Have To Say You Love Me".

6 The Hollies. "Just Like Me", "Searchin'", "Stay", "Just One Look", "I'm Alive", "I Can't Let Go", "Here I Go Again", "Yes I Will", "King Midas in Reverse", "Listen To Me", "Sorry Suzanne", "He Ain't Heavy . . . He's My Brother", "Gasoline Alley Bred", "Jennifer Eccles".

7 Herman's Hermits. "I'm Into Something Good", "Mrs. Brown, You've Got A Lovely Daughter", "I'm Enery The Eighth, I Am", "There's A Kind of Hush, All Over The World", "Years May Come, Years May Go".

8 Adam Faith and the Roulettes. "What Do You Want?", "Johnny Comes Marching Home", "Poor Me", "Someone Else's Baby".

9 The Supremes. "Baby Love", "Where Did Our Love Go?", "Stop In The Name of Love", "Back In My Arms Again", "You Can't Hurry Love", "Up The Ladder To The Roof", "Stoned Love", "Nathan Jones", "Floy Joy".

10 England World Cup football squad. Their one and only record was called "Back Home".

TO QUIZ ON PAGE 64.

1 Mick Ronson.
2 Leo Sayer.
3 Colin Blunstone.
4 Neil Sedaka.
5 David Essex.
6 David Bowie.
7 Jimmy and Randy.
8 Simon, Dee, De Paul.
9 Gary Glitter.
10 Nazareth.
11 Peter Oliver.
12 Madeline Bell.
13 The Zombies.
14 Ian Hunter.
15 Cat Stevens.
16 Thin Lizzy.
17 Mud.
18 Sweet.
19 Barry Green.
20 Marmalade.
21 Strawbs.
22 Barry Blue.
23 Sweet.
24 The Who.
25 Mott The Hoople.
26(a) Ringo Starr.
   (b) "Born to Boogie".
27(a) David Jones.
   (b) Saxophone.
28(a) Shirley Jones.
   (b) Keith.
29 Andy and David.
30 Les Gray, Dave Mount, Rob Davis, Ray Stiles.

Top score, for every answer right, is 33.
If you got 30 or more, you certainly know your pop!
If you got between 20 and 30, you're okay — and very much "with it"!
If you got less than 20, we can only suggest you tune in more often to Top of the Pops — and keep in touch with what's happening in the music field.